Praise for *Magic for Troubled Times*

"Deborah's book offers everything I love in a book about the craft; it's practical and very applicable in today's current world climate, and it will still be relevant for future generations as well. Her writing style is very candid and refreshing."

—Eron Mazza, host of *The Witching hour with Eron Mazza* podcast

"Magic is essential today, especially during difficult times, and *Magic for Troubled Times* gives an accessible blueprint on how to incorporate magic into your coping strategy."

—Chaweon Koo, author of *Spell Bound*

"There is a hunger for books about mental health and resilience that are written from a Pagan perspective, and we should all be grateful that Deborah Castellano is adding to this body of knowledge ... She alternates between coaching readers on the sheer mental fortitude needed to begin to recover and taking a deep dive into a particular esoteric approach to crisis. From hoodoo to ceremonial magic, this book covers everything from aligning oneself with a higher purpose to dealing with people whose gossip is keeping you down."

—Terence P. Ward, author of *Empty Cauldrons*

"Deb Castellano opens every chapter with a window into her life during the height of the pandemic and attempted coup d'état in the United States. It's a bold and tangible display of how the recipes and rituals she provides served her during these uncertain times ... From healing, to money, to fighting back with hexes, this book provides powerful sorcery fit for volatile times."

—Jason Miller, author of *Consorting with Spirits*

"At some point in our lives we all face troubled times ... But, when we go through these difficult or traumatic moments, it helps to have someone to assist you in picking up the pieces ... Reading Deborah Castellano's words evokes that magical auntie who will come over to your house, wipe your tears away with a wet washcloth, help you put away the clothes scattered all over the floor, and give you a spell to do that will magically make you feel that you can face another day. If, like me, you find magic to be a source of healing, you will refer to this book again and again whenever you need to lean on something to get through the tough stuff."

—Madame Pamita, author of *Baba Yaga's Book of Witchcraft* and *The Book of Candle Magic*

"There's no witch I'd rather go through a crisis with than Deb Castellano. Compassionate, wise, and approachable, Deb's latest work is a lifeline for anyone who's been dealt a bad hand of tarot cards. Whatever storm you find yourself in today, it too shall pass; and when it does, you'll be glad you had her on your side."

—Mallorie Vaudoise, author of *Honoring Your Ancestors*

"OG glamour magic goddess, Deborah Castellano, is simply beyond compare. Not only is she a most fabulous auntie witch, who dispenses difficult advice with equal parts compassion and candor, but she's also a devoted partner in crime who will watch your back, straighten your crown, and tell you truthfully if your lipstick is smeared. *Magic for Troubled Times* is a crucial read for savvy witches seeking to keep sane (while still getting what we want) as we navigate our individual paths in this ever-evolving new normal. Read this book. Read it twice. You won't regret it."

—Tara-Love Maguire, coauthor of *Besom, Stang, & Sword*

Magic
FOR
TROUBLED TIMES

© John Minus

About the Author

Deborah Castellano (New Jersey, US) (deborahcastellano.com) is author of *Glamour Magic: The Witchcraft Revolution to Get What You Want* (Llewellyn, 2017) and *Magic for Troubled Times: Rituals, Recipes and Real Talk for Witches* (Llewellyn, 2022). She is an independent maker of ritual perfume and other fineries. In 2006, she founded the first steampunk convention, SalonCon. She enjoys old typewriters and record players, St. Germain, and reality television.

DEBORAH CASTELLANO

Magic
FOR
TROUBLED TIMES

RITUALS, RECIPES,
and REAL TALK for WITCHES

Llewellyn Publications
Woodbury, Minnesota

FIRST EDITION
First Printing, 2022

Book design by Colleen McLaren
Cover design by Shannon McKuhen
Interior Art by Wen Hsu

Llewellyn Publications is a registered trademark of Llewellyn Worldwide Ltd.

Library of Congress Cataloging-in-Publication Data (Pending)
ISBN: 978-0-7387-6989-9

Llewellyn Worldwide Ltd. does not participate in, endorse, or have any authority or responsibility concerning private business transactions between our authors and the public.
   All mail addressed to the author is forwarded but the publisher cannot, unless specifically instructed by the author, give out an address or phone number.
   Any internet references contained in this work are current at publication time, but the publisher cannot guarantee that a specific location will continue to be maintained. Please refer to the publisher's website for links to authors' websites and other sources.

Llewellyn Publications
A Division of Llewellyn Worldwide Ltd.
2143 Wooddale Drive
Woodbury, MN 55125-2989
www.llewellyn.com

Printed in the United States of America

For Logan
Who knew I was writing this book before I did.

Contents

Disclaimer

The material in this book is not intended as a substitute for professional medical or psychological advice, nor is it meant to diagnose, treat, cure, or prevent any illness. Readers assume full responsibility for any result of substances ingested and are therefore strongly recommended to consult medical professionals before undertaking or ingesting anything as described in this book, especially if pregnant. The publisher and the author assume no liability for any injuries caused to the reader that may result from the reader's use of the content contained herein. Common sense is always recommended when contemplating the practices described in this work.

Introduction
Pleased to Meet You, Charmed I'm Sure

What's done cannot be undone.
(Lady Macbeth, *Macbeth* Act V, sc. 1, 63–64)

Whether it's fear of a future misfortune, the remembered pain of a long past wound, or the current open wounds you are attempting to heal, you are here to work through difficulty. Be it divorce, death, sickness, a global pandemic, uncertain financial situations, a rough patch in a relationship, death of a loved one, mental illness, chronic conditions, loss of someone close to you, or whatever else I cannot even fathom that is going on in your life, these hardships have brought you here. It's very likely you aren't doing really well right now. It may feel like everything inside you is a raw nerve and like all your emotions are screaming. You may feel the opposite—like you are dead inside and it's hard to feel much of anything. You may be attempting to ignore your issues by self-medicating and over indulging. It probably feels like nothing will ever be okay again.

Nothing will ever be the same again. But it will (eventually) be okay again. We can't go back to a time where you have not had this trauma happen to you. We can't go backward at all, we're not wired for that. We can only move forward like pawns on a chess board. We will not become rooks moving backwards and forwards (and sideways too) with wild abandon. We weren't made for that.

1

But together, we can move forward. Forward is movement, and movement is power. Sit with that a moment.

Take a breath. Now take another one, a real one. One that goes so deep that it makes you cough up all the sludge in the bottom of your lungs. Take another breath. Are you eating enough? Are you eating things that are good for your body? Are you taking your meds? Are you moving your body? Are you getting some outdoor air? Are you showering and brushing your teeth? Are you drinking enough water? Are you stepping away from your phone, computer, and television? If you aren't doing these things, you can start right now. Take a few extra sips of water, get up to stretch, eat something small, wash your hair, step outside for a moment, take your meds. Make sure you are doing those things. Ask for help from someone you love and trust if you're having difficulty, or talk to a doctor or therapist you can trust. Start here with this; the rest will come with time, practice, and work. If you have the energy, check out the (online) Workbook Community (see page 6 for more information).

This isn't going to be a journey—this is going to be a process. A journey sounds fun, a journey sounds optional, a journey sounds like something that requires pumpkin spice lattes with moody music and a leather-bound book for you to write in. A process is something you need to work on; it's not very optional, it's often not terribly fun, and it requires shadow work, which is enjoyably gothic to imagine but usually more about you staring at the ceiling at 3 a.m. wondering how you got here (and how you get out). It may be just you, your newly washed hair, a glass of water, and emails that you write to yourself. A process doesn't really have a destination most of the time. There's not necessarily a social-media-perfect life waiting for you at the end of this to enjoy without any future hardships. But a process will teach you new things about yourself, help you find the skills that you weren't born with but had to learn slowly and painfully, give you a structure to see what you can do with moving forward using tiny steps, and provide opportunity to start healing. It's not as glossy as a journey, but it's very real and very practical. I hope you will start (or continue) your process with me.

Why You Should Trust Me

First, don't. Or more to the point, don't trust me because I was greenlit to write a few books. I didn't learn magic from books. I learned magic from a very wide assortment of occult (non-gender-specific) aunties. I didn't think this was strange until I met my husband, Jow, who learned magic from books, like a civilized occultist. I soon learned that most occultists and witches (especially authors) learned magic the same way. Eventually, I felt like some kind of strange suburban cousin who was trotted out for street cred in more academic circles. "This is *Deb*. Deb learned magic from *actual people*. This is just as valid as learning from *books*. She is, in fact, familiar with indoor plumbing! Let's hear her hot take!"

The thing is, I have lived in a blue state almost all my life. I went to a very large university where there was a Pagan Alliance group I would attend and eventually lecture for. Witchcraft was taught as part of Women's Studies, which was my concentration along with psychology. There were large annual picnics before there were Prides and various groups were always giving lectures to the Pagan Alliance. I had a very large group of aunties to interact with and was obviously much closer with some aunties than others. I went to a lot of rituals. I led a lot of rituals. I went to a lot of events. I gave a lot of workshops. I'm fluent in a couple of traditions and vaguely conversational in a bunch more. I read a lot of blogs. I wrote for decades on my blog. I'm learning to become fluent in newer social platforms to connect with intergenerational witches.

In my larger witchy circles, I could see what happened if you became isolated, if you didn't think before you banged, if you didn't financially plan, if your mental illness was less treated, if you had poor judgment. My closest aunties would tell me that I shouldn't disengage my critical thinking skills in magic. I should probably ask even more questions. And I did! I was the Worst—I would ask as many questions as a toddler would and then evaluate the answers with any auntie who would put up with it. If I was being particularly irritating, I would be reminded that further research on my own was always an option, as was trying out various magic on my own time. But I was never taught to revere anyone as a teacher or a tradition head—I was taught quite the opposite. Because becoming revered could lead to echo chambers and some really shady practices. My aunties were always very upfront with me about being very human and very capable of mistakes. I was taught that *goddesses* messed up sometimes. I mean, it's all there in almost every pantheon. I was taught to call things out that didn't look or smell right, and I invite you to do the same with me. I do my best to continue to learn and grow. Is it always going to be perfect? Am I never going to say or do anything questionable? Probably not, hard as I try. Are there going to be aspects of this book that won't age well in the next decade? Probably! You *should* question me. You *should* question what I'm trying to teach you. You *should* look at my personal life and consider if that's a good fit for you. You *should* question whether every single thing in this book is for you.

My closest aunties loved a good ritual as much as the next witch and were clever and creative in ritual planning, but they were also incredibly practical-minded. They were *never* going to just hand me a spell. They were never as bossy as I am here in this book because they knew I was a twenty-something who could generously be described as strong-willed, so sensible advice was always carefully slid in over tea and little cakes. It was so deftly done that I never realized I was being Jedi-mind-tricked until I couldn't stop thinking about something an auntie had said.

If I could give you tea and little cakes and slide this part in for all of you, my darlings, I would. Sadly, a book format limits how clever I can be, so you will just have to march through this part and see if any of it sticks with you. Or, skip it. You're captain of your own ship.

For me, the practical and the magical are inextricably linked because that's how I was taught myself. Really, what's the magic going to stick to if you don't fix your daily life? It's presumably mostly broken (or you're reading this in case it gets broken), it's why we're here. You think your goddesses are going to want to help you bend the (goddamn) Universe's will to yours if you won't do the part that's all you and doesn't require them?

None of my aunties would have.

But First, the Part You Hate

This is supposed to be a book about magic, right? There is supposed to be nary a whiff of self-help or boring practical procedure because we're going to magically fix everything together, which should not make it so that you are bothered with actual, dull, day-to-day life introspection and making phone calls (gross). Your heart is broken, your brain is numb, your spirit is asleep, your life is on fire—*just make it stop.*

My darlings, I can't make it stop for myself, let alone for you. I wish I could. I wish I could heal your hearts up and float from house to house, sewing everything back together. We would breathe a sigh of relief together, close our eyes, and sleep knowing everything is fixed. I used to be a nanny, I love this image of being your *Mary Poppins* (who was clearly also a witch) and fixing everything and continuing along my way. But I'm sorry to say, this is going to involve a lot of really squicky phrases like "boundaries," "self-reflection," "possibly seeing a therapist," "daily life," and "doing the work." Yeah, I know. I feel you. As someone who has had her life set aflame like a dumpster fire and has set it aflame herself also like a dumpster fire (and I'm not going to judge you for doing either; both scenarios work for this book), that's super unwelcome to hear. I get it. We're going to do magic (it's still a witchcraft book), but we have to do the daily work, too—the part everyone wants to montage over. It will never be a montage for you—a quick little tale on your way to your best life. You know why? Because you have to slog through it every minute of every day getting to the point where your heart doesn't feel like an open, sucking wound. Some details will blur with time, but this kind of back-breaking work is always really fresh in the memory, in my experience.

But we need something for our magic to stick to, as we just discussed. The Universe will see your hustle and want to help you nudge things along magically because you're doing all the shit work no one wants to do. Your spirits, goddesses, and ancestors see you breaking your back, doing all the hard work, having really unpleasant breakthroughs you didn't want to have, doing all the shadow work, slogging through the laundry and the dishes when you want to lie down and die. They will want to help you, too. And if you're not super into the Higher Power stuff, your subconscious will see all the work you are doing along with your magic and find ways to help you, too. Magic is just high-level arts and crafts projects if you don't have the grit and determination to really change your life. And you *will* need to change your life because it's not an ideal situation to continue indefinitely with most of your life broken AF. It's okay if you need a day or two to sit with that. You're not being graded on recovery speed here.

Invocations

While I will give you invocations in this book to use for your work, if something doesn't resonate with you, don't use it. If it does, do. In either situation, I would recommend not just using the invocations I give. You want to tell the goddesses out loud what offerings you are giving them and why (we call that acting as the "Divine Waitress" who reads off the specials to our goddesses in my grove), as well as offering praise to them that comes from your heart. What that praise may lack in polish will be made up for with sincerity.

The Magic for Troubled Times Workbook: A Shared Online Community

Slogging through your current difficult situation is hard enough, and it's made even harder by your loved ones being unlikely to have unlimited bandwidth to give you to help you through. I've created a community called "The Magic for Troubled Times Workbook" on Facebook for us.[1] I can't promise it will be available forever or will be available by the time you read this book. But it will be a place to ask for advice, gather resources, and just vent. I will be part of the group, but I won't be able to respond to every comment personally. But that's also part of the purpose of this haven, so you have each other to go through this together. You'll be able to form a community where you can work through your difficult times together. It will be a supportive environment where you won't need to be worried about being judged for being a witch or for your gender, preferences in partner(s) selection, economic status, skin color, or abilities physically and emotionally. It won't offer professional help—you'll need professionals for that—but it will offer support. Please feel free to check it out.

---

1. Find the group online at: https://www.facebook.com/groups/978255829643333.

We Make It Up! So What?
That's the Part I Like!

I want you to understand why I teach magic the way I do. I teach this way because it's never just about the magic, not if you're doing it right. Sorry/not sorry. You're probably unsteady on your feet right now with whatever brought you to this book, so taking a little time to orient you in how I do things isn't the worst thing for you to sit with. As discussed previously, you have the divine right to question anything I say. But I want you to know where I'm coming from so you ask the right questions. My background informs how and what and why I teach magically; knowing that will help you figure out why certain things gel for you and other things don't. Not everything will. Not everything *should.*

The part about making it up is a direct quote from a circle sister many moons ago. That sentiment directly encapsulates why my circle never joined a bigger Goddess organization. In this, my circle aunties remain consistent. No one wants to be told what to do, ever, unless it's not blowing candles out with your filthy mouth after rituals. That will be the one thing we all won't do until we collectively all drop dead. I can't even completely remember why, because I am finally reaching that exciting age where the details of my life are now sometimes a bit hazy.

My circle and grove were both embodiments of 1970–90s (depending on if you were an auntie or a youth at the time) of the DIY spirit where rituals were meant to be creative explorations. This was where I was formed as a witch through all of my twenties and a chunk of my thirties. The aunties *also* required having done a decent amount of research about the holiday/goddess/ (the likely) terrible idea.

The mytho-poetic is important and deserves sojourn. It's not all about someone once having done a thing so now we all do that thing. With my own family, my grandmother's recipes were notes to herself, not to us. *What does "cook in a very hot oven" even mean, Grandma? I still don't know.* Recipes change and evolve over time, over access to the internet telling you what "a very hot oven" probably meant, and over someone liking or not liking pine nuts. Rituals and magic are the same. This is where you take someone's notes and make it your own, this is where trails of *your* fingerprints will be found some day.

At the same time, you should have a thoughtful explanation about why you want to do whatever it is you want to do magically. Much like the mytho-poetic needs to make sense when verbally telling a story (or singing it as a song, writing it as a poem, drawing it as a picture, or baking it into your bread), it still needs to make some kind of sense in your magic. My aunties were experienced and seasoned enough to know that we were jumping in really deep puddles. Much like childcare and oyster shucking are easiest for adults who did both as almost-adults, magic works the same way. It's not *impossible* to start any of those endeavors as an actual adult, you're just way more conscious of possible injured children and severed fingers.

This is why we would need to give mini-thesis statements to explain to the aunties about why (probably) no one was going to lose a limb in whatever rit-uals we dreamed up while still young. Circle aunties did less fact checking than grove aunties, but you had to make your ritual executable for everyone at circle, so it sort of balanced out that way. Having your shit nominally together was required either way.

All this is to say that I'm (still) not sure why we always need a huge amount of research in magic after twenty years of practice. Baselines, of course. But past that, still not super sure. Jow would say that's because I was always too busy building Tesla scooters in various aunties' basements out of spare parts that *never* should have run together but would be joyfully ridden around the block with great aplomb. Often, my darlings, for me it was more about the journey and the experience rather than the research past the nominal amount required for auntie fact-checking purposes.

If research makes you feel safe and *your* critical-thinking meter is flashing code red, you always have the option to do more research yourself. You *also* have the option to pass on doing whatever suggested magical act is making you uncomfortable. Consent was something drilled into me in both circle and grove before consent culture even really fully took root in sexual negotiation past *no means no*! Magic should be consensual. You don't like something? You don't want to do something? Guess what? *You don't have to.* Yes, even if a god-dess, spirit, or ancestor is asking you to. Unless you've negotiated a relationship where you're not allowed to say no (and probably don't do that), you can still say no. You are allowed to be Not That Into a Goddess, just like they are allowed to be Not That Into You. Generally speaking, if you are polite but firm, that's all that's needed. Sometimes a bit more is needed, but that's a fun off-topic research project for you to explore.

At the risk of offending secrecy-based traditions, I'm going to go a step further: if someone at a ritual tells you that you *do* have to do whatever magic is setting off your internal Bad Touch radar and that other person is unwilling to negotiate or give you another option that doesn't set off your Bad Touch radar or give you the option to opt out or listen to your concerns, listen to your Bad Touch radar. You should scream, "*No! I said I don't want to do this! I said No!*" And leave immediately. The promise of power and magic should never take away your own power and magic, period.

Now, if you want to build your own Tesla scooter and take apart what I share, go crazy. You just have to be able to handle crashing if you crash. Magic is always a risk, but so is getting out of bed every day. If we've learned anything during this pandemic, it's understanding risk assessment. If you need to re-work any aspect of the rites presented here to be more accessible for yourself in any way, please do. If you have any questions about how to rework audio/visual aspects or any other aspect that isn't accessible to you for whatever reason, please feel free to go to my website as listed and contact me, I will be happy to brainstorm with you.

A final note: I use feminine pronouns and nouns, typically. It's what's comfortable for me. I use these words inclusively. If you identify as a man, a woman, a nonbinary person, or your own spectrum, I include you with these words. If you don't like my chosen words, feel free to substitute your own—it's what I've always done. Words have power, so choose the words that matter to you.

One

Roots

While this small book is being inked with this very specific (global pandemic) time and place at its heart, it's not like if/when there's a vaccine everyone will suddenly become exempt from future hardship. The etchings of this particular moment in time will be on our bones for ages, and these are the ancestral markings that we will leave on future humans.

Sometimes It's a Wish, Sometimes It's a Dead Chicken's Broken Clavicle

I still feel the Great Depression coursing through my body, even though I would not be born for another forty-six years. It settled into the bones of my grandmother who sent it coursing through my mother's veins through her lifetime. My mother, in turn, breathed it into my sister and me. My nephew is now a third-generation American, but the prints of his mother, my mother, and grandmother rest upon his (somewhat spoiled) brow. Our anxiety has been bestowed upon him, especially during the pandemic, a dubious gift at best. We worry, always, about shortages. It's only taken us two generations to resume this particular worry in earnest.

My mother, sister, and I traveled to our ancestral place of origin two summers ago, not knowing what would lay ahead for us two years later. We didn't worry about breathing in our grandmother's air then; we worried if Sicily would be a dog hole. We wondered if we would be too spoiled as Americans to enjoy any of it.

It was a luscious, carefree trip, probably the last one we would ever take with just the three of us. Sicily was so much more than we could have even dreamed of.

The bejeweled blue waters, the saints and goddesses everywhere, the wine that flowed like honey, the rich cannoli cream and blood orange mimosas at breakfast, the ruined temples and the churches with ceilings strewn with astrological movements made us breathless.

I didn't know it then, but I was trying to find pieces of my grandmother's legacy, the only grandparent I ever knew. She left because it was such a poor country. Unification destroyed most of Sicily and the mafias destroyed what was left. She would have enjoyed the ridiculous brunches we got to have together overflowing with cakes, breads, cheeses, yogurts, and dried meats. It was a bounty that was unknown to her growing up during the Great Depression. Her American dream was now nestled into little niches of her terra firma, all led by our handsome, smoking, slouching, Italian tour guide.

I wonder what my grandmother would have thought of us in her homeland and about the pieces of American life we brought with us. My sister and I called my first-generation American mother "Signora No Pesce" while moving from city to city, refusing every scaled creature our motherland was known for. Would she have found my mother wanting for sunning herself on the deck of a private boat and exploring a volcano? Would my grandmother have turned up her nose at my sister for eating cakes with great enthusiasm at breakfast and taking pictures of everything while I lit candles to Mary Magdalene in every church and documented even sacred places? Or, would she have romped alongside us excitedly, teaching us more of the language while laughing and eating everything delicious? She died when I was six, so my memory doesn't have the answers I need for these questions. I remember playing dolls, her little garden, taking naps with her on the couch, everything a child would remember. I think, from everything my mother has told us, she would have been happy, perhaps an occasional small good-natured scolding for eating too much cake and taking pictures inside churches.

Still, we would pose like old movie stars at the temples. We would daydream, looking out the windows, watching the countryside go by and seeing parts of her own country she never got to see. Sicily is now as inconceivable to me as it was before I visited. It feels like a dream from another life. Because it is.

Even as the pandemic seeps into all of our bones to spill into our future ancestors, it's not the only thing we will ever have to endure. We all have abysses we will need to cross at various points in our lives. We have other disasters to expect for ourselves. There will still be upheaval in our political climate, other unexpected illnesses, relationships of all stripes abruptly ending, workplaces dissolving, and the deaths of loved ones. We will experience other substantial shake-ups that break us down, deep dives we never asked to take that sometimes feel more like drowning than diving.

Not Everything Is Evergreen

I am supposed to give you a sense of timelessness when I write for you so that you can read this ten years from now and it will hold up just as well as if you read it yesterday. Everything should feel fresh and nothing should feel dated. In principle, this is a good idea but it's not flawless. Sometimes I'm yelling at characters to just text each other (they can't; texting isn't a thing yet). Sometimes I'm wondering why they're not utilizing online reviews better in a "save our whatever" reality show (they can't, it's not a widely accepted platform yet). Other times I'm cringing extra hard about an author being so earnest but completely missing the mark on an issue of intersectionality (the discourse wasn't there yet because the piece was written fifteen years ago and we've all done a lot of work to grow and change and evolve since then). I think too much evergreen doesn't give you enough of a snapshot of where we are, where I am, right now. It won't give you enough perspective on the heart of this book. It won't let you be forgiving of me for the flaws that this place in time has given me. It won't let you see inside me enough to understand why I can't stop writing this book, even though I've tried to more than a few times.

Today, on April 22, 2020, at 12:12 p.m. there's a pandemic happening throughout the world. Here in New Jersey, we're the second worst hit in the United States. It is impossible to say what tomorrow will bring. Today, we're not supposed to leave our houses unless it's essential. Essential is limited to fixing something at home, to buying food for our families, to mailing things, missions of that nature. That's about it. We have to wear masks while we do this. I've learned during this time that I am a very moist breather. I'm still trying to get used to it. I'm grateful to have a few masks but it's a transition to need to wear a mask to leave the house.

Many of us, myself included, are unemployed for the foreseeable future. Maybe we will have jobs again if/when we've flattened the curve enough to safely go back to some semblance of regular life, or maybe we won't. Small businesses (like the one I work for) have been hit particularly hard during this time.

Some of us need to work from home on endless Zoom meetings while juggling children who have to be wrestled into being educated. Some of us are like my husband, Jow, who is an essential employee. Some, like him, expected to be essential. Some didn't expect to be considered essential but are pushing forward as best they can. Jow is a nurse; he knew he would be essential. He got drafted almost right out of nursing school into a stepdown unit for the virus. As you can imagine, that's very different than, "yell at older people to take their meds and maybe learn to put in an IV," which is the actual job he agreed to do. Per our governor, people were supposed to go to his facility when they recovered enough to not need a ventilator at the hospital but still required supervision. But they sent cases that didn't fit that criteria and not everyone there got better. The morgue in his facility wasn't big enough to accommodate the people who had passed. Now, there's a protocol they have to follow to keep the bodies intact until there's space for them.

Everything is canceled: weddings, funerals as we know them, vacations, festivals, walks in the park, happy hour with friends, swimming, mani-pedis, waxing and hair color, pet grooming, gym class, otherwise manageable problems, bitching about everyday life, brunch, dinner parties, proms, graduation, birthdays. No one gets anything right now.

We don't know what regular life will look like after the curve is somewhat flattened. No one knows what it will look like in the fall when the virus is likely to spread again. Right now, if we're lucky, we're kept in a safe womb in our homes where we are given money, where there's food and supplies, and we are left to our own devices. Some of us are less lucky; money is uncertain, we're forced to shelter with an abusive partner, or we have other chronic conditions to worry about. Some of us are too depressed and anxious to do much past the bare minimum. Some of us are trying to propel ourselves into our best lives through elaborate cooking and baking rituals, extensive curricula for children at home, brainstorming start-ups, or working on diet and exercise. Which one we identify with often depends on the time of day and how we slept the night before. It's a very specific time and place right now. No one knows what to do really, but we're marching forward anyway.

Later in this pandemic, we have other worries. We worry about what police officers are actually supposed to do in our communities, especially when it comes to people of color. They aren't *supposed* to kneel on people's necks for non-violent crimes. They aren't *supposed* to break into people's houses when it's the wrong address and shoot someone to death while she's sleeping. They're not *supposed* to be proactively arresting people. We worry about our civil rights through the legal system, we worry about the democratic process of selecting our leadership. We worry and worry and worry.

When the world is turned sideways, everything in you goes with it. It's hard not to be engulfed in waves of sorrow and helplessness. For a time, that's exactly what you should do—be engulfed and only do what is immediately necessary. Whether for days, weeks, or months depends on you and the circumstance you find yourself in. There comes a point where you need to get up again. The problem is, it can be hard to know what to do when you are standing upright again, wobbling.

Find the Ground Under Your Feet

You've had a terrible shock. Whatever grief-laden event has brought you here has come with a soul-shaking blow. Everything you once knew to be true is now up for cross-examination. It's imperative that you spend some time holding space for this dramatic shift to your insides. Whether you lost your spouse to death or divorce, whether your workplace has unexpectedly closed its doors, whether there's a large rift in your family, whether you've had a difficult medical diagnosis; whatever it is, you need some time. This time will help you find the ground you stand on. Once you've managed to feel the ground beneath your feet, you'll be able to start rooting yourself into this new terrain. Your roots will, at first, be very small and very tentative so that if the new place where you are standing is too unsteady for growing bigger roots, you can keep moving until you find solid ground. Then, you can begin slowly growing more roots until your roots are bigger and stronger. When you have strong roots in your new life, it will become more possible for you to make changes as you move forward. As your new life progresses and your roots are now sturdy, you will be able to handle new upheaval. But right now, you need to work on current upheavals that have brought you to your present life.

During this retreat, you only need to do what is essential:

- Keep your body, dishes, and clothing clean.

- Continue with any meds you may take, eat food, drink water, and attempt a regular sleep schedule.

- Care for any children or pets you may have (or find trusted care for them if you are not able).

- Show up to work if applicable, or request time off or leave (if your situation can qualify for paid or unpaid leave).

Usually, adults around you will understand that you need more time for yourself than you usually would. Children won't understand, of course, but firm boundaries help during this time with children and adults alike. A firm bedtime and, perhaps, a little extra screen time for kids will help give you some time to process your situation. If your situation allows for play dates or some time for your kids to spend with your family or other trusted people in your life, that can help too. With adults, you can be much more specific. You can enforce your boundaries by saying something like, "Hey, Adult Who is Asking Me for Something I Don't Have the Bandwidth to Give. As you know, I'm going through My Situation. I can't commit to social plans/non-urgent projects at work/volunteer work/whatever activity that's being proposed that I can reasonably say no to without dire consequence given my situation. Thank you for being understanding, I'll let you know when/if I'm ready to resume my previous activities."

You may be thinking to yourself that's fine for me to say but your situation doesn't allow for you to step back. Maybe not. But with any large change in circumstance, there's much more sympathy and empathy for your particular circumstance (your spouse is having an affair, your mother was diagnosed with stage four cancer, your kid is having psychological difficulties, you are now performing two people's jobs at your workplace, your roof will need to be completely replaced, your particular set of troubles) when it first happens than six months to a year from now when you are a burnt-out shell of a human being. At the beginning of a disaster, everyone wants to help. Everyone wants to be understanding and kind, but that patience is limited and the shot clock on that patience starts the moment your difficult events begin. Say no to as much as you can in the beginning, because that's when the other people in your life will have you in mind. *Of course she can't chair the bake sale, her dad just died two weeks ago.* It's human nature for better or worse (often worse) to want your fellow humans to get on with their lives. Most people aren't thinking, *oh of course she can't chair the bake sale, her dad died a year and a half ago.* It's not a pretty thought, but it is the way the world usually works, unfortunately. This is why it's so important to be present with your grief, sadness, anger, anxiety, and/or depression as soon as possible. Don't put it off. If I've learned anything from experiencing my own losses and strife throughout my forty-something years on this earth, it's that the only way out is through. When you work to be present with your troubles and work your way through them emotionally, physically (because there's a physical component too), intellectually, and spiritually, you begin to actually work on starting to heal. It's a long, tedious process that no one wants to engage with. But it's a *shorter* tedious process when you actually *do* engage with it as quickly as possible and hold space for the process.

During your time contemplating your crisis, take some long walks and do some yoga, if possible. Try to connect with your physical body because that's how you start to repair some of this damage. Yoga with Adrienne on YouTube offers yoga for small spaces, beginners, people with mobility issues, broken hearts, and yes, even the pandemic. I'm sure you can find a match for yourself; the internet is broad and vast and full of people with tutorials.

Write your experience down in a way that is meaningful to you. Step away from social media as much as possible. Talk to people you love and trust. Connect with your goddesses in some way. Drink tea. Grieve. Complete the tasks you're obligated to, and then work on your shit. Be gentle with yourself, allow yourself some space for a few distractions and bad habits. You're not going to be perfect during this time because you're impaired. You're going to make some bad choices. But try to limit those bad choices to things you can manage. It may not be a great time to make giant life changes like having a partner cohabitate with you, moving across the country, or becoming a vegan. These things will be there for you past the initial shock period of time. You don't have to rush into anything. Take time to be in your cocoon to heal and grow. Read nourishing books, pin your best future life, start therapy, talk to a spiritual life coach, work on ongoing projects in baking or cooking or sewing or gardening or making art.

You cannot stay in your cocoon forever; eventually, life must go on. This is the tricky part—how long one needs to stay in one's cocoon really varies from person to person and whatever difficult experience you're going through. Some experiences take less time to process than others. Some people are more resilient and will recover faster, but it's not a race. You don't get a prize for being able to shovel trauma faster. When the ground feels solid under your feet again, more often than not, when you have some good days for no reason, it's probably time to move onto the next step, which is coming out of your cocoon.

A therapist can also help with this process. TalkSpace offers online therapy at reasonable prices and OpenPathCollective offers both in-person and online therapy services for those who are struggling financially. The internet is a valuable tool to find assistance. Search "text-based therapy" or "low cost therapy in my area." If you have a specific area you need assistance with (divorce, death, childhood trauma, an assault, issues that you need specific sensitivity to like recovery, being a witch, sexual identity, or gender identity), add those keywords to your search.

If you are ready to start coming out of your cocoon, don't freak out. You don't have to do it all at once. You *shouldn't* do it all at once. Pick a few small things to work on every day. An early stage cocoon list for a week can look something like:

- Clear off the dining room table.

- Go for coffee with a friend or have coffee together online.

- Do a thirty-minute work out.

- Cook dinner at home (this can be mac and cheese and turkey corn dogs from Trader Joe's). You're not being graded on creative content, just that you've accomplished it.

If you try to immediately jump back into your "old" life, you'll become overwhelmed and give up. Not to be indelicate, but also, you *can't* go back to your old life, just like a butterfly can't become a caterpillar again. And that's okay! What you *can* do is move forward. You can start thinking about what you would like to accomplish for yourself: maybe this year is the year you learn to knit and start figuring out how to accomplish that. If you want to learn to knit, you can ask a friend to show you how, you can get some yarn and needles, you can watch YouTube tutorials, you can set a goal to learn to knit a scarf within three months.

Now that your inner ant farm has been unceremoniously given a good hard shake, what do you want to do differently going forward? You can't be a caterpillar again, you're a butterfly now, like it or not. So, what do you want as a new butterfly? Are there habits you want to change? Maybe there are relationships you want to work on or reconfigure, a new way to earn income, a dream you've always wanted to pursue? Do you want to make changes to your home, your diet, or your physical body? It's easy to want to rush this step, to try using your new wings to fly a hundred miles, but slow and steady is easier to manage. Take small steps. Don't set yourself up for disappointment in the knitting scenario by telling yourself you'll have a whole sweater by the end of winter—start with the scarf. The scarf can be done with one kind of stitch and doesn't require you to figure out arm and neck holes. The scarf doesn't require thousands of yards of yarn. The scarf is a good beginner's project. The sweater is a bitter, expensive path that will (probably, though not definitely) lead to failure and disappointment. If this is not an area where you excel, there's lots of great resources that can help you figure this out. Marie Kondo teaches you how to take apart your entire house in a fairly reasonable manner. If you want to read some books on putting your life back together, Mark Manson is accessible, as is Sarah Knight. For deeper dives, you also can read Brené Brown and Glennon Doyle. Feel free to research your little heart out to find what works for you.

Before the Great Pandemic Never-ending Rounds of Layoffs, my work wardrobe had become designed for a few things: *Can I crawl on the copy room floor to fix the copier with some dignity? Are my boobs super covered up? Is it a comfortable dress made from a mostly natural fiber that can be mixed and*

matched? This isn't terribly exciting, frankly. It's functional, sure, but not exciting. I knew I would be out of a job until at least July in late March 2020. And
then darkness and dragons, who knows. I still don't. I put together a narrative
about what will happen in July for my own sanity's sake, but it is not grounded
in fact. I could spend this unprecedented amount of free time chewing my own
tail to a bloody stump *or* I can accept that this is happening. If you are chewing
your tail to a bloody stump, that's a valid choice, too ... for a little while, at least.
After a while, it's not good for you or your tail, which is where a professional
could help. For me to accept that this is happening, I needed to start struc-
turing my new life. I struggle with self-structure. Part of why I always wind up
working for someone else is that it always seems easier ... and it is! I just show
up, do my job, get treats, and go home.

Opting to just find another authority figure wasn't going to be an option
here, so I started with the most obvious thing. I did the full KonMari closet
meditation. This approach may be helpful to you as well. I took out all of my
clothes along with my workout clothes drawer for good measure and started
mixing them up. Now that I didn't have to worry about appearing buttoned
up enough for finance, what did I want to wear? The longer that quarantine
has gone on, the more creative I've gotten. An earlier spring look for my walk
was a soft, floor-length gray duster; a black cotton tank-top; black cotton leggings; thigh-high, gray-striped socks over the leggings; ballet flats; and my rabbit Parrish Relic necklace. Obviously, that's not a look that would fly in finance.
Later-summer, pandemic working outside looks include a bikini top and linen
pants with brightly colored silicone rings for my fingers and big faux Jackie O
sunglasses.

I've also had to get creative to manage my personal femme outer glamour during this stage of pandemic—learning to do my own roots, waxing, and
nails, which may be something you will also need to consider if your financial
situation has changed. I started working on what my schedule would look like:
a smoothie first thing in the morning, a long walk outside if the weather was
good or yoga indoors if it wasn't, taking care of the dishes and other housework
that couldn't be ignored, working on my shop or writing, and then making dinner and spending time with Jow. It's taken me some time to get here, probably
close to six weeks.

Part of this process is finding some gentleness for yourself. Very few people can do anything perfectly immediately. It takes practice and refinement. It takes a little time. It takes a willingness to try out your new butterfly wings a few times and face planting onto a hard surface. It doesn't feel great, but face planting is how we get better.

You need to step forward, my loves. I know you are afraid. I know this isn't what you asked for. I know how heavy and smothering your sorrow, your anxiety, your depression, your pain, is. You have to step forward anyway. It doesn't matter if it was of your own making or a twist of fate, how you got here. It matters what you do with it, now that you're here.

Take time to work this out for yourself. Feel your way through until you own the ground beneath your feet again, until you are sure-footed, clearheaded and your heart starts to open up again. As I've said before in my earlier blogging, you don't want to be doing magic while you can't find the ground beneath you. Tiny roots first, magic later.

The world reshaping itself around you makes it *impossible* for you to make sound decisions. This reshaping is a magic in and of itself. Perhaps the most neutral magic of them all—it doesn't care if it makes you happy or miserable. It's happening. Until you find solid ground, it's changing too fast for you to affect it. Wheel of Fortuna, every time. So, don't. Don't decide anything. Let the world re-form enough around you that you can own the solid ground you stand on again before you do anything. When you start to feel like you're standing on solid ground, start considering what practical actions you need to take. Start taking these actions and wait another week before you even divine (through tarot, your dreams, goddesses and spirits, runes, tea leaves, radiomancy, whatever your thing is) if it's right to do magic. Will you have enough control over your will and your magical ability in a state of shock? No. You will not. If you really want your magic to stick and to count, you will need to summon enough self-control to wait until you have complete mastery over your will and be able to competently cast.

Grounding and centering magic is the exception. You can work on grounding and centering whenever you want. They are prerequisites to taking on other kinds of magic. You *can* skip that part, but I don't recommend it. The rest, wait until you trust yourself to be able to control your own will. None of this is going anywhere; it will be here when you get back, pinkie swear.

For me, this tumultuous time of worldwide unrest and hardship has been an exile of a different kind. For those of you familiar with my blog, you know I talk a lot about exile because I find it to be a fairly flexible concept. I became interested in the idea of exile because in the Middle Ages, it happened to royals and people of influence all the time. "Exile" could mean being locked up in the Tower to think about why you were bad or at a country estate where someone was unlucky enough to get to serve as your jailer and hostess (Mary Queen of Scots was a *notoriously* expensive "guest"). You could need to sail to France. You could be with the bones of your ancestors in Westminster Abbey. Sometimes, you were eating two-day-old fish and selling your gold plate like Queen Catherine of Aragon, or you were still drinking expensive wine and sewing with gold embroidery floss like Mary Queen of Scots. Sometimes you were allowed outside to run and fall in love with your fellow jailed royal teens like Queen Elizabeth I. More than anything, exile meant either being kept out of the game at court or your hands were so bound that you couldn't move anything anyway. Mostly, you waited. To add insult to injury during this current troubled time you're experiencing, it probably comes with a heaping helping of exile.

What do exiled royals from the Middle Ages have to do with *you*, right? You live in New Jersey (hey girl hey!), drink Starbucks like it's your job, dictate texts into your iPhone, imbibe St. Germain cocktails, and drive a slightly beat-up car—what could that possibly have to do with medieval tales of exiled queens?

Your exile could come in many forms during your troubled times. You could be exiled from your family (possibly even your children) right now due to choices you made. You could be exiled from in-laws you had come to love and trust; you could be exiled from your chosen family due to deciding to do something that they did not care for. You could be feeling exiled from your own body if it's changed (or not changed) in a way that you don't like. You may need to work in an occupation that doesn't suit you and drains you of your energy, that's an exile, too. You may be suddenly without means (or you are learning right now) in exile due to your difficult situation, a change in finance or status. Maybe you're not holed up in a crypt claiming sanctuary hoping for the tides to turn, but we all know studio apartments that have felt that way (or moving back home with parents can have a certain crypt vibe). Most of us know what it feels like to suddenly be without means, what it feels like when social circles turn against us or when we are left without help. You may as well claim your crown in this place of despair, this Ten of Swords place. It's yours. No one can take it from you.

Not for long, anyway.

Two
Grounding

Now, let's get started on centering you in your practice to start working through your particular set of troubled times so that eventually, you can bloom again. If you have ever picked up a beginner's magical book, you are probably at least a little familiar with the concept of grounding. I've never personally been hugely into grounding or meditation, but even I will have to grudgingly admit that a small amount of both is required to manage the anxiety that comes with whatever trauma you are living through currently. You will also need some form of grounding to be able to focus your will for performing magic. For instance, if you lost your job, being able to focus on grounding yourself can help you figure out what job you'll want next. If you just lost a loved one, grounding can help you plan the memorial rites or go through their possessions or be present with your grief. If you've been through a natural disaster, grounding can help you figure out the ins and outs of dealing with your insurance claim, as well as if you want to rebuild or start somewhere else.

When you experience trauma, it's not uncommon for part of your spirit to want to disassociate from the experience. It's usually part of your lower spirit; your id, your fetch, your primal self who wants to cut bait and take off. With enough practice, grounding will help you focus on being present with the moment you are experiencing in your process, instead of distracting yourself permanently with the emotions of the moment. Your emotions are *always* valid, but they aren't always the most helpful. Learning to ground during heightened emotional states requires an incredible amount of discipline. Grounding during the beginning or the end of a ritual can feel optional (…just me?), but grounding yourself into the moment through your will is a completely magical act. It's a lot harder to do while experiencing feelings of being overwhelmed, anxious, sad, in despair, depressed, unmotivated, angry, or any other feelings you may be feeling right now. Grounding yourself while feeling neutral or positive emotions is easy. Grounding yourself while feeling strong negative emotions is not easy.

Being present during a crisis is really difficult. We are offered up so many delicious distractions on a silver platter—excessive drinking (booze, caffeine), smoking, illicit substances, scrolling on phones, bingeing on television, involving yourself in drama that doesn't actually matter, overeating, or undereating. Whatever your numbing agent of choice, I bet this is where you expect me to self-righteously talk about how I don't even *watch* television. Oh no. I *love* to get numb. I could scroll forever; I could happily rosé as many days away as I could; I can name every Real Housewife's husband, and in my heyday, I could solo eat half a dozen donuts and a whole pizza. (Probably not on the same day. *Probably.*) Everything is so easy when you're numb. You don't have to feel anything too hard; you don't have to try at anything too hard; you can excuse your need for it really easily. You worked a really long day! The kids didn't stop fighting until you put them to bed! Dealing with this disaster is really hard! And if all of your social circles love to numb themselves too, you *definitely* earned that marathon scrolling session on Insta. It's even harder because we're actively encouraged in prosperous nations to not deal with our difficulties. If your mom died, you are *entitled* to three pieces of cheesecake. If your partner cheated on you and then divorced you, obviously you *need* to get under three new sex partners over the course of a week.

Being present is really difficult in this modern age, which is why it's so important. Everything around us invites us to disengage. But if you want to do any of the exciting occult work and are invested in it actually working, you need to learn to do this part first. Remember, we aren't striving for perfection but we are striving to feel the ground beneath us. You need to feel that ground under your feet for you to be able to be present. You need to be present to do magic. You also need to be present to deal with your trauma because the only way out is through, unfortunately.

Your lower spirit is an easy way to refer to whatever that thing is inside of us that tries to scare us into inaction when life gets really difficult. You see why we say spirit. If you have a better word, feel free to use it. Your spirit can't really get too far outside your body generally in this kind of situation, so it will act like a dog trying to snap her leash. There's a lot of straining, a lot of jumping, a lot of barking. That barking will likely sound like screaming in your head or an endless unproductive cycle of anxiety.

Grounding is teaching your lower spirit to heal so you can figure out how to do something productive with it. Whether it's focusing on magic, actually pulling yourself together enough to do the laundry or taking a walk outside to figure out what to do, grounding will help you get to that next step. With enough practice, it will stop your internal screaming, for a short period of time at least. It could be seconds, possibly minutes, possibly hours, possibly days. That part depends on how much screaming you've got going on and how often you can work on your grounding practice. Like everything else in life, practice is what improves your natural innate ability. Natural innate ability gives you an easier start, but it doesn't mean you'll make it to the finish line. Practice is what gets you to be able to actually ground consistently.

As someone who lives with her fair share of internal screaming, grounding is a worthwhile pursuit but takes time and practice. You know how most of us don't have an innate ability to tie a complicated tie knot correctly the first time, or to use liquid eyeliner to do a really beautiful cat's eye right the first time? It takes work and effort to achieve success. It takes accepting that it's probably going to look like a hot mess the first few times. In this specific case, it will not fix all of your anxiety and uncertainty on the first try. If you know how to ground already but often opt out, it may take a few attempts of opting back in before it actually works.

Some people get really uptight about sitting in a specific position for this. Often in life, when I need to ground the most, I'm dealing with phones ringing off the hook and clients bitching about my inability to control time and space for them so I'm on the bounce. Sometimes I'm caught in an anxiety loop when I'm attempting to sleep, so I'm lying down. It doesn't matter if you are staring into the abyss of the supplies closet hoping to manifest paperclips. Or, if your kids are yelling at the top of their lungs attempting to drive you to the brink of madness. For me, grounding works in any of those physical positions. But then I'm twenty years into my grounding practice, whether I wanted to be or not.

The critical first step of grounding is recognizing that you need to. This is harder than it sounds when part of your brain is chanting at high speed, *everything is fine, everything is okay, this is no big deal* and the other part of your brain can't see how you're going to make it through this moment without someone's blood on your hands. Maybe prison is more of a viable option than you previously thought?

Take a couple of slow, deep breaths. Remind yourself that your lower spirit needs to stay put in your body while dealing with this stress. Remind yourself that being present right now is important. Ask yourself, "What am I feeling?" This might take a moment to figure out. If you can do this outside, great. If not, just making yourself do this is the important part.

Imagine yourself growing roots through the bottom of your feet burrowing through your socks and your shoes. Keep shooting your roots down past the crummy carpet, the building's foundation, the clay underneath the foundation, and keep digging with your roots until you get to soft, fragrant, deep, loamy soil. Steady yourself there for a moment with your roots in the earth. Pull your own energy up through your roots until the energy gets to the bottom of your feet again. Now pull that energy up through your body. Past your ankles, your knees, your thighs, your junk, your stomach, your ribcage, your heart, your throat, your mouth, and your eyes, and then imagine that energy becoming branches of a tree growing out of your head. The branches reach up to the sky until they twine around the stars. Then draw that energy all the way back down into your roots in the earth. Pull that energy all the way back up and out through your branches into the sky. Repeat this until you feel present in your body again.

Realigning Yourself

When you feel overwhelmed, it can feel challenging to want to do a fussy ritual; I know for me it is. This is where connecting to the primordial goddess energy of the Universe can be helpful. In Hinduism, the primordial goddess energy is what makes the Universe do things. Goddess energy achieves this goal within a particular belief structure. God energy is Being. For example, Parvati *does* and Shiva *is*. Parvati always wants to go go go and do all the dishes and make all the biryani and do all the laundry. Shiva just wants to hang out in the cremation grounds and chill with his cremation grounds bros. But Parvati needs to take a bath and relax sometimes, too, and Shiva needs to sort out demon-related issues that he has helped facilitate due to technicalities. You need both kinds of energy in your life, to both accomplish things and chill, which is why both energies are accessible to all genders.

For the sake of this form of grounding, we're going to focus on doing and the primordial goddess energy aligned with the ebbs and flows of the Universe. We're going to do a mantra (a sentence that will help you focus and ground yourself) using a mala (a string of 108 beads similar to a rosary), which is called *japa* practice (an active form of meditation).

You can make a mala yourself; there are plenty of tutorials available or you can buy a mala either via Etsy, Amazon, or your local Indian grocery store, such as a Patel Brothers. When holding your mala, you hold it in your right hand using your thumb and middle fingers. You *don't* use your pointer finger. You pull the mala toward you with those fingers. Say your mantra with each bead.

This is how you hold mala beads.

The mantra suggested for this grounding practice is: *Ahdi Shaki Nah Moh Nah Moh;* in English, "Primordial Universe (Herself), I bow to thee!" You can use whichever language you feel more comfortable with. If you find another mantra that you would prefer to use that makes you feel grounded, use that instead.

You want to bow to the Primordial Universe (Herself) because she's calling all the shots anyway, and she takes equal pleasure in your suffering and your success. With that in mind and by bowing to her, you're acknowledging that you can only control so much in this life. You likely are not able to control the courts, death, illness, workplace politics, your family's irritating habits, or your financial situation as much as you would like, so it can be grounding to formally acknowledge this fact. I find it takes away some of my stress. It also never hurts to tell the Universe that you know she's the ultimate Maya player, the game of illusions that the goddesses play. The rough equivalent is the modern children's game Snakes and Ladders or Chutes and Ladders. While you're there, you can also mention to the Universe that it would be really helpful for you if she could make more ladders for you than snakes.

Not Every Goddess Has a Name

Once upon a time, before there were names, there was an assemblage of goddesses who lived beneath the earth, the Sisters Below. They were happy in their warm, earthy little chalets, surrounded by radicles and their fiery small familiars. Their hearths were always cozy with the bread they would bake, the books they would read, and the life they would spin on their spinning wheel. They lived mostly in solitude and were glad for it. They preferred to leave the larger suffering that was the cause of larger pleasures to their mortal Sisters Above.

But that did not mean that they were deaf to the suffering of their Sisters Above. If the Sisters Above were struck with great enough suffering, the Sisters Below would fall to their knees on the floors of their houses, to the dirt in the forests outside their homes, to the bustling streets that made the roofs of their underground residences. The Sisters Above gave great cries of anguish, despair, disbelief, bereavement, failure, and loss that never failed to reach the Sisters Below. Sometimes in a whisper, sometimes in a roar. Sometimes the Sisters Above would curl in the roots of trees, under hedges, in fields, on their kitchen floors, on the floor in a bathroom stall, or under their beds, and they would howl or murmur their deepest hurts to their Sisters Below living under the loamy soil.

The Sisters Above would picture their Sisters Below, calm, with teacups in hand, sketches and notes in small books on a table, listening to their pleading. The Sisters Above would press their hands, their feet, their hearts, their heads to their most accessible connection to the Sisters Below through their floors and the soil to feed them all of their unhappiness, their restlessness, their discontent. This was the bargain the Sisters Above agreed to. They knew this. The exchange of larger joys for larger sorrows. But sometimes it was too much to bear. It was often a worthy bargain, though never an easy bargain.

And when it was too much to bear, they would give all of this to their Sisters Below. The Sisters Below would spin this heartache into the breath of life on their spinning wheels. The Sisters Below would weave this pain and grief into roots of flowers, herbs, and mushrooms on their looms. The Sisters Below would bake this longing and resentment into their bread; steep this melancholy into their tea so that it sustained them. They would roll this misery and discontentment into small toys for their familiars to play with. They would turn this fretfulness and misery into patches for their skirts and boots and roofs.

For this is what bound the sisters to each other, this unending cycle of anguish and distress being made new. Being made beautiful. Being made useful. The Sisters Above could not exist without the Sisters Below and the Sisters Below could not exist without the Sisters Above.

Sisters Above, when your afflictions are too heavy to hold, when your part of the bargain feels too great to manage, give it to your Sisters Below. Let them turn your difficulties, trials, and burdens into something as important as you are. Call your tribulations within yourself. Name each one to yourself and when you know each one by name, pull that poisonous energy from yourself. See each piece as a thorn or your own creation. Pull each piece from where it resides in your body with your dominant hand and place it in your nondominant hand. Your worry for your sister's happiness? Feel that anxiety, let it crystallize. Where does that live? Is it in your throat? Let it become a thorn. Is it made of specific words or sounds? Is it a color? Pull that thorn from your throat. Place it in your nondominant hand. Your grief over the passing over your mother? Let that sadness wash over you and feel it. Where does it live? Is it in your heart? Let it become a thorn. Pull it out. Place it in your nondominant hand. Your rage over a recent breakup or divorce? Let that anger flow through you and experience it. Where does it live? Is it in your belly? Let it become a thorn. Pull it out. Place it in your nondominant hand. Your insecurity about not being enough for your career, your family, your obligations? Feel that insecurity, let it well up in you and feel it. Let it become a thorn. Pull it out. Keep pulling thorns out of yourself until there are no more thorns left. Go outside. Put your hands to the earth and then ask the Sisters Below to take all of your thorns. Feel all of that negative energy that has crystallized into your hand as thorns sink deep within the earth. Keep your hands to the earth until you can't feel the thorns in your hands either physically, emotionally, or spiritually. If it's a safe space to do so, say whatever you need to say. Howl if you need to and don't think the cops will be called. Whisper if it's a more public space and wait until it's late at night. When all of your thorns have been taken by the Sisters Below and you have a feeling or an omen of some kind that your thorns have been taken (you can always use tarot for this), lie on the ground.

Thank the Sisters Below for taking your thorns. You can either use hand sanitizer to wash your hands clean and write words or sigils on yourself to protect yourself, or you can bring out a bowl and wash your hands with warm water, a little sage oil, and a good bit of salt. When everything bubbles up within you again and it feels like it's too much to carry, do this ritual again. Remember that this is reciprocal work—you are giving something to the Sisters Below to work with and they are giving you a release from all that you hold onto. If it feels right, make small offerings of bread, salt, mushrooms, or crystals as you work together. You can look for the Sisters in dreams and visions to see what they are creating. You can talk to them about their day and your day. You can visit them to thank them for days where your burden is light and kiss your fingertips and place them to the earth. Everyone is always willing to do much more for someone who shows them care and attention, and the Sisters Below are no different.

You can release yourself from some of the trauma you are carrying. Nothing makes everything all better, just as Sarah said in *The Craft*. But a little better is still more than completely terrible without any respite. Use your magic to heal yourself; it's why you have it. You can bring yourself luck, love, money, protection, power, vengeance—all of these things are part of your magic. Working on healing yourself puts you in a better place to receive all the other aspects you want. You won't be completely healed; none of us are. But a few scars are much better than a gaping chest wound. We're not striving for perfection—we're striving to be mended.

Three
Sustenance

One of the most difficult parts of pandemic has been occasional food shortages. Sometimes it made sense. Yeast was impossible to find for the first couple months because everyone wanted to pretend that we were home for some kind of staycation instead of trying to avoid contagion. Somewhere in there, melatonin became really difficult to get, usually when the death toll was rising and there was political unrest. Whole chickens were sometimes hard to get, as were canned goods such as beans at other times. Sometimes it didn't make any sense at all, like no mozzarella cheese could be found anywhere local to me for a week. I have no idea what that was about. Recently, there's been a Patrón XO Café shortage; I can't find it anywhere. I logically know I do not actually need Patrón XO Café, but having been a creature alive for all her life in the land of milk and honey, this is still a hard concept for me.

I had been blessed in this lifetime to not live with food shortages until this moment, and I found it incredibly stressful to not know what I would be able to get and where, needing to do a whole bunny trail of shops. I had been doing pick up at the grocery store prior to the pandemic. Jow and I were both working full time, but now that wasn't happening for love or money for quite a few months. It felt very surreal to be standing outside various shops, waiting to be allowed into the grocery store, and then not being sure what would even be there. It was a strange time where so much effort was being put into food—acquiring it, storing it properly, and then much more time cooking it. Very little food was wasted during this time in our house, and we were much more creative with leftovers because there was always the fear that there would be whole categories of food wiped out at the door and we would be without. We have this ugly blue plastic step stool that we very extravagantly refer to as the chef's stool. If one of us is cooking, the other will often sit on the chef's stool to direct cooking and to gossip. I came to use the chef's stool to sit in front of the refrigerator, so that all our food would be carefully arranged so that nothing would go off or go to waste as I meal planned. We've reached a point in the pandemic where food shortage is not much of a fear anymore, but it's changed the way I look at food and some of my eating habits as well.

You Need to Eat (So It's Okay to Cheat)

You're just starting to be grounded and getting ready to heal. Food is a really key part to this process and likely something you're struggling with right now. Cooking is magical alchemy and you need to do it eventually anyway. The casserole brigade will only last for so long. It's *always* okay to cheat when it comes to food. By that I mean change the recipe with wild abandon. You want to use full-fat whatever? Go crazy. You want to use reduced fat? That's fine too. You need more animal protein? Great, add it. You hate bacon? Take it out. You only have the energy for box stock and pre chopped vegetables? Fine by me. Whatever you need to do to get food into you works. For me, cooking can give me a sense of control over my life again during difficult times; it's a chance to creatively do something I need to do anyway. Even if cooking is not usually your thing, I invite you to try a few recipes, if nothing else, it will confirm that you still do not like cooking in this new life. It's a simple way for you to do magic, too. You can add basil to a recipe for more money, a bay leaf for success, or cinnamon to speed things up. Just putting your hands over your food with intention for the meal adds magic to eating and supporting your physical body.

No matter where you are in your process of moving forward into your new life, you will need to eat. You may be having trouble getting food in you at all and may be having difficulty finding the energy to cook. I've included very simple recipes in the less complicated recipe section. You may be starting to get to the point where you would like to have slightly more process-intensive recipes or welcome the distraction of cooking. I've included recipes for that, too. These recipes are also focused on comfort while still giving you the option for fresh vegetables and herbs, and animal proteins, so it includes a lot of soups and pasta as those foods tend to be affordable and soothing as well as easy to modify for dietary restrictions and personal preferences.

Less Complicated Recipes

A Stock Recipe for the Tired, New, and Afraid

1 rotisserie chicken (eat the parts you want and put the rest into the stock, especially the bones. There's usually a bit of gelatin in the chicken bag, put that in the stock.)

Mirepoix (a mix of pre-chopped carrots, celery, and onion)

1 lemon, juiced

1 head garlic (whole thing)

1 bay leaf

Salt to taste

Put all the ingredients in the biggest pot you have. Fill with water. Put the pot on the lowest setting your stove has for at least three hours. More time is better, but we have to start somewhere. Refrigerate overnight. The next day, use a strainer to skim off fat, chicken, vegetables, etc.

Put the liquid back on the stove for another hour or two on medium-low to reduce for richness. Freeze or refrigerate.

Beef Marrow Stock

1 marrow bone (about a pound)

¼ C red wine

1 onion (whole thing)

1 carrot

A few mushrooms (dried mushrooms work well)

Fresh parsley

1 head garlic (whole thing)

Fresh thyme

1 bay leaf

Salt and pepper to taste

Put everything in the biggest pot you have. Fill with water. Put the pot on the lowest setting your stove has for at least three hours. More time is better, but we have to start somewhere. Eight to ten hours is ideal. Then refrigerate overnight. The next day, use a strainer to skim off the fat, bones, vegetables, etc.

Put the liquid back on the stove for another hour or two on medium-low to reduce for richness. Freeze or refrigerate.

Vegetable Stock

2 T miso paste

A large handful of dried mushrooms

1 bunch leeks

1 parsnip

1 stalk celery

1 carrot

1 rutabaga

1 bay leaf

1 bunch thyme

1 T butter (or olive oil)

Put everything in the biggest pot you have. Fill with water. Put the pot on the lowest setting your stove has for at least three hours. More time is better, but we have to start somewhere. Then refrigerate overnight. The next day, use a strainer to skim out vegetables.

Put the liquid on the stove again for another hour or two on medium-low to reduce for richness. Freeze or refrigerate.

Burnt Garlic Oil

2 full heads of garlic, peeled and chopped

1 ginger root, chopped

½ C sesame oil

Sauté the garlic and the ginger until everything is burnt black. Let cool. Put everything in a blender or food processor and blend until smooth. Refrigerate. This oil can be added to soups or used as a marinade.

Banana Peanut Butter Smoothie

1 C of milk of your choice

2 scoops protein powder of choice

2 T peanut butter

1 whole banana

Put everything in a blender and blend until smooth.

Black Forest Oatmeal

1 C water or milk of your choice

¼ C frozen cherries

1 C quick oats, plain

Salt to taste

Sweetener to taste

1 T cocoa powder

1 T chocolate chips

Bring water or milk to a boil with the frozen cherries. Add the oats, salt, sweetener, cocoa powder, and chocolate chips. Cook on medium low for about ten minutes, stirring regularly.

Yogurt Parfait Bowl

¼ C quick oats

1 t chocolate chips or cacao nibs

½ C berries or bananas (can be frozen)

1 C your choice of yogurt

Cinnamon, to taste

Honey, to taste

The first layer in your bowl is the quick oats and chocolate chips. Next, the fruit. On top is the yogurt with the cinnamon and honey drizzled to taste.

Beet and Beef Soup

    1 pound beef stew meat

    6 C beef stock

    4 beets, shredded (A food processor is great for this, if available)

    A bag of shredded cabbage

    1 T dried dill

    ½ C unfiltered apple cider vinegar

    Smoked paprika

    Salt to taste

    ¼ C fresh parsley, chopped

    Sour cream, for garnish

    Fresh rye bread

Brown the stew meat. Put everything in a pot but the parsley, sour cream, and bread. Simmer on low heat for 1 to 2 hours. Garnish with parsley and sour cream, serve with bread. As leftovers, it's even better.

Pumpkin Curry Soup

    2 T butter

    3 T all-purpose flour

    2 T curry powder

    4 C vegetable stock

    1 (29 ounce) can pumpkin (NOT pumpkin pie filling)

    2 T soy sauce

    1 T molasses

    Salt and pepper to taste

    ¾ C plain yogurt

2 T raw pumpkin seeds (garnish)

3 strips of crisp bacon, crumbled (optional garnish)

Put everything but the garnishes and the yogurt in a large pot. Heat on medium heat for fifteen minutes. Add yogurt, and cook for another 10 minutes on low heat. Garnish with pumpkin seeds and bacon.

Pasta con Parsley e Dill

1 box pasta elbows

4 T butter

½ C grated Parmesan cheese

1 C fresh chopped parsley

1 C fresh chopped dill

Salt and pepper to taste

Cook pasta according to directions and drain. Add the rest of the ingredients. Serve.

Tea Egg

Small mason jar

3 T soy sauce

1 t Chinese Five Spice Powder

1 hard-boiled egg, peeled

¼ C Lapsang souchong tea

Add the soy sauce and Chinese Five Spice Powder in the jar. Add the egg. Fill the jar the rest of the way with the tea. Put the lid on. Shake. Refrigerate overnight. It is ready to eat the next day.

Scotch Eggs

½ pound loose sausage, seasoned to taste

2 hard-boiled eggs, peeled

Olive oil

Wrap the sausage around the hard-boiled egg so it looks like a bigger ball. Heat some olive oil in a frying pan on medium heat. Add the eggs. Cook until browned, about 10 minutes, depending on thickness.

Ginger Vegetable Soup

    4 C mushroom or chicken stock

    1 small yellow onion, chopped

    4–10 cloves garlic (to taste), crushed and chopped

    1 carrot, grated

    4–8 fresh shiitake mushrooms, sliced with stems removed

    1–3 T grated fresh ginger, to taste

    1 fresh lemon, juiced

    3 T chopped fresh parsley

Bring the broth, onion, garlic, carrot, mushrooms, and ginger to a slow boil. Reduce the heat and simmer covered on low for 15 minutes or until the veggies are soft. Remove from heat, add the lemon juice and parsley. Cover and steep for 5 minutes.

More Complicated Recipes

Roasted Chicken Dinner

    1 white tealight

    1 whole 3- to 5-pound chicken completely defrosted, ideally room temperature

    2 T butter

    ½ bunch of thyme

    ½ lemon

    1 bulb of garlic, cut in half (unpeeled!)

    1 container of fresh brussels sprouts (or some other roastable vegetable)

    1 packet of powder chicken gravy

Salt and pepper to taste

Roasting pan

Take three deep breaths to focus. As you are lighting the candle say, "In the Name of God Herself, Please bless me with your presence here in my hearth," or whatever you like. The goal here is to make the everyday sacred.

Preheat your oven to 425° F. Remove your chicken from its packaging and remove any plastic or string. Now, this is where you're going to get really close to your chicken. The cavity is located between its legs. Remove whatever jewelry is on your hand and wrist and reach into that cavity and pull out whatever treats they've stuffed in there (usually the neck and the gizzards) and pull them out. Put them aside.

Feeling close to your chicken? Good. Now you are going to loosen the skin by the cavity so that the skin is not attached to the meat on the top of the breast and bottom of the chicken. Carefully stuff about half a teaspoon of butter in between the skin and the meat on each side without ripping the skin. I'm lazy and can never find my pastry brush, so I rub butter with my fingers all over the chicken. Use as little or as much as you want.

Wash your hands with soap and concentrate on making what you're doing a little hand-washing purification. You can put a little table salt in your hands while washing them to make that so.

Take your thyme and run it over the candle. Touch the thyme to your heart and say, "In the Name of God Herself, who is so beautifully crowned, keep my home safe and sound. Make me strong, make me bright, keep me within your light."

Put the thyme inside the cavity.

Take your garlic halves and run them over the candle. Touch the garlic halves to your heart and say, "In the Name of God Herself, even keeled, keep me safe within your shield." Put them inside the cavity.

Take your lemon half and run it over the candle. Touch the lemon half to your heart and say, "God Herself up above, infuse me with your love." Put it inside the cavity.

Say, "By my strong and mighty will, I will keep running up that hill."

Put the chicken into your roasting pan. Try to tuck the wings under as best as you can. Trim your brussels sprouts and surround the chicken with them. Cook for one hour, but make sure the juices run clear. After you're done cooking, either let the candle burn out by itself or extinguish with a candle snuffer saying, "God Herself, I thank you for your presence."

Fish out brussels sprouts. Carve the chicken in the roasting pan if possible, so you have the juices. Remove chicken pieces and carcass (with stuffed ingredients) from the pan. Add the chicken gravy powder and about half a cup of water. Stir until not lumpy and pour into a gravy boat.

Put the carcass, neck, and gizzards into your Crock-Pot. Add whatever odds and ends you have in your fridge—limp parsley, old carrots that haven't gone off yet, celery that's lying around not doing anything, etc. No chopping is needed. Fill the Crock-Pot with water. Cook on low until morning and strain. Now you have stock.

Grain Bowl

1 C grains of your choice, cooked

½ C shiitake mushrooms, de-stemmed and sliced

½ C sliced brussels sprouts

½ C of your protein of choice, cooked

1 T rice seasoning or black sesame seeds

Sesame oil, for drizzling

Salt, to taste

Put the grains at the bottom of the bowl. Season and sauté the vegetables for about seven minutes. Add to the bowl. Add the protein. Sprinkle with sesame seeds and oil.

Smoked Duck Noodle Soup

2 cartons chicken stock or 8 cups homemade

1 small head napa cabbage, chopped

1 carton shiitake mushrooms, chopped and stems removed

2 T miso paste

2 T sake or rice vinegar

1 package soba noodles

1 T Chinese Five Spice powder

¼ C soy sauce

1 package smoked duck (if you can't get smoked duck, pork belly or firm tofu are good substitutes)

2 tea eggs, for garnish

1 t chili paste (optional)

1 T burnt garlic oil, for garnish (optional)

Pickled plums, for garnish (optional)

Diced green onion, for garnish (optional)

Bring vegetables, miso paste, sake, spice, and stock to a boil. Add soba noodles, cook for seven minutes. Add the duck and the garnishes.

Vegetable Pasta

2 large zucchinis, sliced into planks

1 small bunch carrots, sliced into planks

1 carton large portobello mushroom caps, sliced

2 T olive oil

1 box pasta shells

3 pieces of pancetta, drained and diced (optional)

1 C milk

1 T butter

½ stick reduced fat cream cheese

¼ C shredded Parmesan cheese

¼ C fresh basil sliced into ribbons

¼ C fresh parsley, chopped

½ C sliced sun-dried tomatoes

Salt and pepper to taste

Set your oven to 200° F. Toss zucchini, carrots, and mushrooms with olive oil, and salt and pepper. Spread over a baking sheet and slow roast for about two hours. In the last 20 minutes, cook pasta according to the directions on the box. Put pancetta, milk, butter, cream cheese, Parmesan cheese, basil, parsley, sun-dried tomatoes, and salt and pepper to taste in a pot. Put on low heat and cook for about 20 minutes. To the pot, add the cooked pasta and vegetables.

Baked Potato Quiche and Salad

2 C baby kale

1 baking potato

Olive oil

6 mushrooms, sliced

1 onion, sliced

Smoked paprika (to taste)

Salt (to taste)

1 egg

3 slices ham

½ slice provolone

1 T cream or milk

Wilt the kale for 30 seconds in the microwave. Put aside. Using a fork or knife, poke a few holes in the potato. Microwave the potato for 2 minutes. Turn the potato over. Microwave for another 2 minutes. Remove carefully and let cool.

In a skillet, heat some oil. Put in the mushrooms and onion, and add salt and smoked paprika with two pieces of the ham, diced. Sauté until golden and add to wilted greens.

Hollow out the potato so that it's still got a solid bottom, a potato boat. Put aside the scooped-out potato. Sprinkle salt and paprika to the potato boat. Put the cheese in. Melt the cheese on the potato in a 350° F oven for about 10 minutes.

Mash the scooped out potato with the cream, a little olive oil, and salt and smoked paprika. Form it into a patty. Add that patty to the skillet and cook until golden. Add to wilted greens.

Mix the egg, smoked paprika, salt, and one ham slice, diced. Pour into the potato boat. Cook for 5 to 10 minutes, until crusty.

Chicken Cauliflower Rice

One head fresh or frozen cauliflower, riced (I like frozen better)

4 boneless skinless chicken breasts or thighs

½ C plain yogurt

½ lime, juiced

4 T biryani paste, divided

4 t ghee

4 T chicken stock

2 T tikka masala spice mix

Small bag fresh peas

1 carton mushrooms, sliced

Salt (to taste)

The night before, in a freezer bag marinade the chicken with the yogurt, the lime, a tablespoon of the biryani paste, and salt. In a big pan on medium heat, melt the ghee. Add the chicken to the pan and brown it. (Discard the marinade and bag.) Next, add the rest of the ingredients and cook it on low for about a half hour.

Cassoulet

1 T butter

1 large onion, diced

1 carton baby bella mushrooms

4 cloves garlic, minced

½ C dry white wine

1 carrot, diced

1 parsnip, diced

1 can cannellini beans, rinsed and drained

1 can chickpeas, rinsed and drained

Large can of diced tomatoes, undrained

1 C stock

1 t smoked paprika

Bundle of fresh thyme, rosemary, parsley, and a dried bay leaf

Salt and pepper to taste

¼ C seasoned panko breadcrumbs

¼ C grated cheese

4 pieces of bacon (optional)

Preheat the oven to 350° F. If you are using bacon, put the bacon in a large pot on medium heat on the stove. Drain some of the grease out of the pot. Add butter, onions, mushrooms, and then the garlic. When everything is browned, add the white wine and scrape the bottom of the pot. Add the rest of the ingredients except the breadcrumbs and grated cheese. Simmer uncovered on low heat for at least an hour. Put the cassoulet into a casserole pan. Top with breadcrumbs and grated cheese. Bake for 30 minutes.

Homemade Chocolate Chip Protein Waffle (or Muffins)

1 extra ripe banana, mashed

1 t honey

½ t vanilla extract

½ t cinnamon

½ C oats, ground (I use a coffee grinder)

1 scoop protein powder

2 T vanilla almond milk

1 dash salt

1 t mini chocolate chips

Heat the waffle iron to medium high. Mix the honey, vanilla extract, salt, and cinnamon into the banana. Add the oats and protein powder. Stir. Add the almond milk. Stir for a batter consistency. Grease your waffle iron. Cook the waffle for five minutes. It will be a little soft and floppy, but it will slide out.

For muffins, add a tablespoon of olive oil and one egg to the mixture. Preheat the oven to 350° F. Fill muffin tins ¾ full. Bake for twenty minutes or until a toothpick comes out clean.

Jow's Beef Stew

    1 T olive oil

    Flour for dredging

    1 pound stew meat

    1 large onion, diced

    1 carton sliced mushrooms

    2 large carrots, diced

    2 large stalks of celery, diced

    1 carton beef stock or 4 C homemade beef stock

    ½ bag frozen peas

    2 cans of Italian Stewed Tomatoes (with juice)

    1 heaping handful of barley

    ¼ C red wine

    1 t garlic powder

    1 bay leaf

    Salt and pepper to taste

You will need a large stock pot for this, as it makes about 12 servings. Heat oil in the stock pot. Dredge the stew meat in the flour and brown the meat with the onion, mushrooms, carrots, and celery. Then add the rest of the ingredients except for the barley. Let simmer at medium heat for 1 hour. Then add barley and cook for another 45 minutes to an hour, stirring occasionally to keep barley from sticking to the bottom of the pan. Serve.

Four
Healing

We are now seven months into the pandemic. When pandemic first hit, most of us spent a lot of time dreamily considering the things we would do once we got back to real life, because this would last maybe six weeks and then everything would be back to normal. I wanted to visit My Favorite Houseguest (MFH) and insist on an afternoon fire with roasted Italian chestnuts; I would take Jow to the Morgan Library and pretend to be Belle in a Beast's best library; I would go to a con with Mx. Spice and dress up, flirt, drink, and dance. I would have one of my parties for all of my friends at my house and stay in the kitchen and let it wash over me from there. I would go back to work at my corporate gig and resume my position in the copy room, singing songs to Mary Magdalene. The resuming of life as it was now seems just as far away as the idea of the pandemic going on for seven months with no end in sight. We may get a vaccine in 2021, but no one is sure. We don't know what the side effects will be, how well it will work, and who will get access to it. A party in my tiny house seems as impossible as growing wings and flying.

I had been recently elected by all sides of the family to oversee my nephew's virtual days at school. Since he is nine, self-directed isn't really a thing that's happening yet. I arrange for virtual coding lessons through Minecraft with MFH, I make sure he does some yoga, I try to remember math and mythology, I oversee his Zoom band instruction. Jow had always been his favorite by far. I was always too bossy and scolding, but now he is eating my cooking, laughing at my jokes,

51

and pleased with my whimsy. We have become cozy with each other, one of my biggest blessings during this arduous time.

Recently, I was driving home from my sister's house on a highway. It's raining and I'm thinking about if I feel like going to the gym for an outdoor spin class in the wind tunnel of my gym's parking lot, or if I want to pretend going to Target is the same thing. An accident happens in front of me, in my lane. One car hits the other. It happens so fast. I slam on my brakes and I start spinning. I see the 18-wheeler truck and I think *oh god, this cannot seriously be how I die. Slamming into a truck thinking about Target.* I keep spinning and try to steer. I think, *oh dear god, please just don't let me hurt anyone else. Please. Please.* For a moment I think I can course correct. That I will be lucky, that my heart will be pounding and I will be safe and my car will be safe and this will just be a little story I tell off hand.

But it's not.

I can hit another car or I can hit the divider. I don't want to hurt anyone else. I hit the divider. Hard. Hard enough that my air bag goes off. I had never been in a car accident where the air bag went off before. I'm shaking and crying really hard. Usually tears are like blood from a stone for me, but I'm completely freaked out. My right hand hurts very badly, it's burned a little from the air-bag. My chest is throbbing, I will have really terrible bruises where my seat belt was, though they heal well perhaps due to all the collagen I had been drinking for my photo shoot for this book a week prior. Vanity as a saving grace. There's an awful smell from the air bag. I call my mom. I don't want to call Jow, he's still on shift. I want him to be able to concentrate. I note the time so I know when his shift will be over and I can tell him. I start texting A1 because I know she can be calm about this. I dread telling everyone else. Everyone is already torqued up from pandemic, this isn't going to help. I can't think about that yet. I have to concentrate on my next steps. I limp my car to the shoulder.

There are a lot of accidents on the highway, so the trooper is very brusque with me, a warm up to being shoved into the tow truck and dumped at a convenience store to wait for my mom, outside in the rain, everything still throbbing in pain. I call my doctor and make an appointment. I wait for my mother. By the time the insurance adjuster on the phone flatly tells me I am to blame for this, I'm pretty numb to shitty dudes in authority telling me everything is my fault. I have been crying in front of all of them, especially for some reason when I say I didn't want to hurt anyone. That is impossible to get out of my mouth without sobbing. I still feel it in me if I think about it too hard because I don't think of myself that way. I think of myself as a survivor, as a queen often in exile. I don't think of myself as a soft girl who apparently would literally rather die than hurt another person. But under the hard layers, there it is. And it's humiliating to be this sobbing mess in front of these terrible dudes. Because I would also rather die than be exposed like this in front of them. But I don't get to choose and that's another layer of awful. It just keeps happening. All the calls, all the paperwork, all the running from place to place. All of these men, almost all of them acting like this was some flighty choice I made, like a deer running into traffic.

While I start to untangle all the paperwork that goes with this, the 2020 presidential election is soon under way. It had the biggest voter turnout in history, likely because we were allowed to vote by mail. But voting by mail meant that it would take a long time to count all the votes. We knew that going in; we told ourselves we were prepared to wait. We all knew that this election would take a long time to figure out. Knowing didn't stop what it actually felt like to wait. Almost no one I knew was sleeping. I was sleeping very soundly due to the shock and trauma I had just gone through. I think it was hard to viscerally understand what it would be like to be holding this vigil for days on end about who would be deciding what happens to us on a federal level (and local levels as well) for however long the pandemic would go on. So, we waited. We waited and we waited. I remember thinking that I had found in (pandemic) exile a patience that I didn't know I had. It sprang from a well within me that ran so much deeper than I ever thought it would. An unexpected gift that has served me better than almost anything during pandemic.

That patience didn't stop the emotions though. I felt like a frog in a pot, churning and waiting, slowly being heated. Waiting to see what happens with my car. Waiting to see what the election count is. Waiting to see what the next four years of my life holds in this country that I love so fiercely but makes me despair so much. Waiting to see if I qualify for a medical cannabis card in New Jersey, because fuck it, my car is totaled, they're saying it could take all month to get the results to the election, and we've legalized cannabis in New Jersey this election. What's more 2020 than being laid off with a husband on the front lines, a totaled-out car, and deciding to at least getting one's med card out of all of this?

I was outlining this chapter outside of a local coffee house, drinking a mocha hot chocolate with Jow and NurseCat while they studied various things. My email pinged and I read a *New York Times* article that the election had finally been decided, thanks to Philly. We breathe for a moment, feeling that thrill of cautious hope run through us.

I remember what Holly Black said once as an author—no one knows how you're feeling when you're writing something unless you explicitly say so. I find that really soothing sometimes. That I can write something beautiful and no one will know I felt like I was at the bottom of a well when I wrote it. I felt that way writing most of my last book.

The (Goddamn) Universe (Herself) sometimes thinks of herself as a comedian. When I blithely sent my outline to my editor and included this chapter about healing, I was thinking about you, not me. I didn't expect to still be healing myself as I write this.

Having that personal connection to one's art is often viewed as a good thing in this modern life, but at forty-one years old, I've had enough trauma to heal from throughout the course of my life. Definitely enough to write this book prior to the accident. I didn't really need any more, thanks. But that's part of this book, too. The unlit path the dark of the woods strewn with rocks and sticks that none of us asked to be on but find ourselves running down with bloodied bare feet anyway.

It's difficult to share this experience, it's so new. It's so fresh. Remembering what it was like shuddering in my car, trying to figure out if I was hurt badly, the terrible smell of things burning, the rain, the feeling of being engulfed in darkness, the sound of my own ragged breath, realizing how close I was to being grievously injured at the very least, possibly killed at the very worst is a lot to process. The impact happened so fast that I have no memory of the moment, just the memory of the sound.

Allowing myself to be seen as healing too is also difficult. I don't want to be healing. I want to be composed with soothing cool hands to seamlessly guide you through your process, but life doesn't work that way. So instead, I will show you all my scars. I lost my dad at eighteen and we had a complicated relationship. I lost my beloved uncle long before any of us were ready to be without him, I went through a crushing divorce that was a surprise to me, which brought me to the edge of bankruptcy. I have fibromyalgia, depression, anxiety. I struggle with not being present especially as a trauma response. If given the consequence-free option to drown it all in food, intoxicants, and reality television, *I would choose that choice every single goddamn time.*

Many of my scars are healed or mostly healed. This one from the accident is still slathered in ointment, oozing gross pus everywhere. It's okay to get new scars when unexpected events in life happen; you don't always have a choice in the matter. It's okay to get new scars from making choices that turned out to be wrong for you. It's okay to get new scars from mistakes. It's okay to have difficult things happen in your life, whether it's a global pandemic, an unexpected loss, an unexpected trauma, or even a difficult event that you expected. It's okay to have scars. It's okay to still be healing. It's okay that it's a process. It's okay for life to be imperfect. Together, we can heal ourselves and hold each other up while we work through our own journeys. The (Online) Workbook Community is a great place for this. We can light a tealight for each other when we are struggling in our own dark forests. It only takes one tealight for there to be a light of some kind. One spark. One spark to start the bonfire for others to see and for you to know that you'll be okay.

Find Your Own Way

We all do magic differently. I think it's easy to believe otherwise through books or group ritual when it seems like many people do magic roughly the same way. For most of my twenties, I thought this was what kept me from being a Serious Witch—I didn't read enough books, I didn't mediate for hours, I was not a good visual thinker. Retrospectively, this is sort of hilarious given that my grove and circle were such gorgeous examples of creativity and challenging accepted magical norms. I'm still not sure if I am a Serious Witch twenty years later, but I am certainly competent in doing magic.

It's so easy to get caught up in doing it "right"—these mudras! These words! This order! This passage from this book! A confession: as a youth, I secretly wished I could just get my circle and my grove to get into lockstep with what

I was trying to do as a sometimes priestess. I had worked so hard, goddamnit! Just do what I tell you! But I was always gently, but firmly, told that that way leads to madness. And you know what? It does. Participation should be consensual, you can't control the weather in other people's heads in ritual or outside of ritual, just like no one can control the weather in your head but you. If you are dealing with a breakup or job loss, you may not be in the mood for five hours of chanting. It may be *exactly* what you need, but you may not feel like it. Maybe doing it will bring a revelation to you. Maybe you need to opt out. It's a mystery. Sometimes you won't know until you're there at the ritual and need an escape hatch or you feel significantly better than you did before you went.

That's not to say you shouldn't have a plan (and a back-up plan and a back-up back-up plan…) or that you don't need to do research or some play-testing as we have previously discussed. But what you don't want, especially while you are dealing with your current difficulty, is to lose the opportunity to be creative. You are already dealing with drudgery, misery, and unhappiness. The last thing you need to do is to suck all the joy out of your magic as well. You want to be open to inspiration, to change the format slightly because it better fits that night, to speak from your heart instead of a piece of paper, using your words and not mine.

Your magic probably looks different than mine. It *should* look different than mine. Your magic, your intention, your dedication are what will start you on the journey to heal yourself. It's going to be your work that moves you forward and opens magical and mundane doors for you. Don't lose sight of that. If it was as easy as saying the right words from the right books, using the right components on the right day at the right time, the world would be knee-deep in wildly successful, prosperous, happy witches who never ever have anything bad happen to them. You're more clever than that, you know this starts inside you. The rest is just a compass that helps you find your way.

Creating Sacred Sanctuary

"Sacred" is defined as *connected to the goddesses and so deserving veneration.* "Healing" is defined as *the process of making or becoming sound or healthy again.* "Sanctuary" is defined as *a place of refuge or safety.*

Let's think about this.

We are working to become sound again, to feel the ground beneath our feet, to light that one spark in the dark during this troubled time. You know what's a lot of work? Everything I just said in that sentence. Making doctors' appointments to pay for tests we don't particularly want, trying to have a civil conversation with our exes to save money with the lawyers, enforcing limited screen time for the kids with limited (or no) wine for us, slogging to the gym for a class where the first few minutes will be miserable, visiting very sick loved ones in the hospital, and on and on and on. It's exhausting! Sometimes, we all need a space to just chill out for a hot minute. We need tiny sanctuaries to call our own where we can rest and heal. That's what we're going to work to create together here, both with our physical space if that's available to us and energetically (which is available to all of us, thankfully).

There's obvious sacred space, like an altar dedicated to your goddesses. Then there's less obvious sacred space, like my (former?) copy room. When I first started in this position, the copy room looked, well, sort of institutional. And not in a good way. Everyone in my office acted like it was really unusual for me to care about that space. I understood that—for most of them, it's a very transitional space where they only spend a couple minutes a day. But I could spend up to ten hours there. While my basic comforts were seen to (having a nice floor mat for my feet, a phone in close range, everything neatly organized), my less basic comforts were not. I didn't know what to do; as much as I thought of it as "my" space, it was really everyone's space even though I spent the most time there.

Eventually, I had a new supervisor who also agreed that it seemed to be a depressing space for one to spend most of the day. She encouraged me to make it my own and helped me do that—she brought me artwork and blown glass and a ZZ plant which can survive in artificial light just fine. I started to play music I liked there on my phone. It felt much more homey for me after that, as opposed to being sent to time out.

Think about a place outside your home and workplace that feels sacred to you. It can be a public space like a museum or a private place like a favorite friend's home. What makes it feel sacred to you? Is it because of the energy? The artwork? The plant life? The layout of the space? Make some notes, draw some sketches, start a Pinterest board, listen to music, whatever you like to do when you are thinking about issues involving space.

Before we get too far in, let's start by unpacking how much privilege is involved in the concept of private personal space. Some of you may have had to boomerang back home and are currently residing in your childhood domicile that your parents have forbidden you to make changes to. Some of you may be living in intentionally small living spaces that may have seemed like a better idea pre-pandemic. Some of you may be sharing one room with roommates because living in a city is expensive. Some of you might be living in dorms. There are lots of reasons for why you may not have full range to immediately create a whole room that is a sanctuary space for yourself, including many, very real financial reasons because all the empires are burning right now. You may be closeted about being a witch to your housemates, you may just be a very private person. All of these reasons are valid. If you *do* have a whole room you can turn into a sanctuary space, how luxurious! Please share *all* the details in the (Online) Workbook Community.

Can you think of a space where you spend a lot of time? At work? At home? Let's talk about making this space sacred. Could you make items to make this area feel more sacred to you? Handmade always adds something extra to a space. But not all of us have the luxury of time to do so. You could also go to thrift shops for tiny delicate cordial glasses, discount stores for the perfect soy candle, or skim your local neighborhood marketplace for free items through an app for plant clippings, cloth, small cutting boards that can work as altars, and interesting statuary.

If you already consider this space sacred, what little touches could you add to it to make it feel more sacred to you? Maybe a candle or a crystal or a peacock feather—whatever speaks to you for healing. If there is no space for additional objects, that's more than fine. You know what also counts? Giving that space a good cleaning. For some, that may sound scary and intimidating. It doesn't have to be—taking ten minutes to wipe down your work or home area with some Clorox wipes (or baking soda and vinegar or whatever you prefer to use) counts. Once you've added a few little touches and/or cleaned, consider what you want to do to cleanse the space. For example, you could spray the carpet with some rosemary water made from spring water and a few drops of rosemary essential oil, you could make a sound using some bells, you could touch the objects in your space and ask your objects to let go of negative energy that others have brought to them, you could sprinkle some salt, you could light a candle. Doing this mindfully is the important part—keeping your intention to make the space sacred for your day-to-day life rituals is the key.

If you don't already consider this space sacred, think about space you *do* find sacred. How could you translate that into your current space? Take your time with this—create a Pinterest board to look at for inspiration and consider asking friends and family for suggestions on the aspects you find sacred and how to bring them into your space. Keep in mind budget for any new acquisitions. This *does not* mean spending a lot of money and it *definitely* does not mean spending a lot of money you don't have. My most special cordial glasses were purchased for a quarter each at a thrift store. Is there anything you could make yourself? It's even more special if you worked on your sacred objects yourself. Do you need to potentially reconfigure the space for the energy to flow better? Once you've figured out what you need, remember you may not get it all right the first time. I've had to meditate on altar cloths, for example, sometimes for a few days at a time, trying this and that until I found the perfect pieces. Once everything has settled, feel free to cleanse the space as outlined above.

Also remember: if cleansing isn't your thing, that's okay too. You can simply thank the objects in your sacred space for doing their jobs and welcome the new objects into your space or do whatever works best for you.

Creating a Working/Healing Altar Space

A working/healing altar space is a small space in your home that you can use as a visual focus for your healing work. It's not dedicated to a particular goddess, but it's more of a workspace for you. The space doesn't need to be large; my working altar space is part of a small kitchen counter where my bread machine lives. I have a small tealight hearth there and I put down slate tiles on top of said Formica counter so I can burn candles directly on the tiles and make chalk markings with wild abandon.

If space is an issue, you could use a small tin like an Altoids tin and keep it tucked away in a drawer or your purse or your pocket. You could also keep it on your bedside table or on a bookshelf. Think tiny: you can keep things like a small sachet with rosemary, salt, and lavender in it, or a matchstick-sized piece of clear quartz crystal, or it can carry a charm that reminds you of healing, a Cornish game hen's wishbone—whatever feels right to you. You can line the inside of the box with fabric or paint over the outside with sigils that are magical to you.

If you are less pressed for space, carefully consider where you want to put your working/healing space and why. I put mine in the kitchen because it's an active space and I'm often there working anyway, so I may as well do the magical Work there too. I have also used small television trays as working space as well. What will you put on your working space? Chalk to use to draw symbols on it? Your grandfather's compass? A small piece of artwork or garland that you've created? A tiny silver bowl filled with salt? A vase you love but have never been able to use? What feels right to you? Why? You don't have to create this quickly; you're not going to be magically all healed if you put it up faster.

Some magical work takes much longer than others. Healing is an excellent example of that. You won't do one (or even possibly ten) rituals and have everything fall neatly back into place. It's a marathon, not a sprint. Healing magical work (along with trudging through the day-to-day healing work) is a process. It will take as long as it takes, so settle in. What rituals are *excellent* for—keeping yourself focused on healing grief, shock, pain, and difficulty. Rituals are your formal declaration of intention to the Universe. You are formally marking that you want her attention on this matter of healing, as well as marking your own intention to do all the difficult work that is required both magically and in daily life to start your healing process. Yes, you will often see direct indications that your magic and your daily work are having an effect with enough time, patience, and attention. Other times, you won't; sometimes it's just doing the work without validation because you know it's important. Many times it will be this. Everyone is really supportive about your first trip to the gym or your first recovery meeting or for your first week of being unemployed, but after a while, their attention moves on and it's up to you to continue grinding because it's important to you, not for the validation.

What can you do that will consecrate the healing altar space for yourself? I've drawn sigils in silver sharpie, I've anointed my working altar space with a sprig of thyme and rose water, I've slowly passed a candle over the space, I've sprinkled dirt from outside my home on the space, I've used my own breath to consecrate space. Whatever feels right for you and your healing intention is a good way to go here. Spend a couple minutes a day with this altar you've created to remind yourself of your intention of healing. You can say your specific intention out loud, you can ask for help in specific aspects of your healing process, or you can share victories that you've won and difficult things you've accomplished toward healing with your goddesses and ancestors. You can light a tealight and sit quietly considering what your next step is on your route toward healing.

Creating an Inner Sanctuary

If your current exile in your troubled times makes it so that your income and physical space are limited, creating an inner sanctuary can be a balm for your wearied spirit. Exile is trying for even the most resilient and most motivated among us. In addition to limited physical space and income, other aspects in your life may be limited as well. You may have needed to sell some of your favorite household goods, your access to luxuries such as your favorite yoga studio and grooming service may be limited; you may have needed to scale down on purchases of books, candles, and incense, clothing, cosmetics, coffee, and dinner out. It can be easy to get weighed down by what you don't have or can't get. Making a gratitude list daily during financially sparse times can help you appreciate what you have and what you have access to. That gratitude can make you feel a bit less burdened, anxious, or depressed, which can open you to new ideas, new magical workings, new creative pursuits. These are the things that make exile much more bearable.

If it makes you feel a little sad (or a lot sad) because you wish you had unlimited income and space, building your internal sanctuary is your chance to do things exactly as you want to. You want an underwater palace? You want a giant sprawling mansion? You want a cliffside cottage? Go crazy. It doesn't matter how exiled you are, Sister Queen. The only limit to your internal shrine is your imagination. Money and space are no object. This is where you get to have everything *exactly* the way you want it. It's likely the only place that will be the case for all of us, so really luxuriate in it.

But first, before we start creating your inner sanctuary, let's talk about my adaption of what Josephine McCarthy recommended in her Master class at the first Magickal Women Conference in London because it's an excellent starting place. Before you go to sleep at night, picture yourself walking through your house. By doing this, you're training yourself to notice details. You want to notice in your mind's eye all the tiny details—the pictures on your walls, your rugs, the books on your bookshelves, the items on your altars and shrines, the color of your dish towels, your shower curtain, your appliances, and electronics. This is really challenging for those of us who aren't visual thinkers but it's even more important for us to get good at this before making an inner sanctuary. It's okay if you don't see this really visually, but you will develop a sense for how you experience this kind of magic. Keep walking through your house until your recollection of it becomes really detailed: all the titles of the books on your walls, all the colors used in the artwork on the walls, the flavors of incense you keep, the clothes in your closet. You don't have to rush through this; there's no prize for doing this part fastest. You want it to stick. Start doing this when you're in other places, such as at work during a free moment or sitting outside in a park or at a kid's swim meet. You want to be able to call this up with as much detail as possible, regardless of your actual physical location.

Keep walking through your house until you start sensing other beings however you sense them—through words, visually seeing them, sounds, feelings/vibrations, whatever works for you. We are defining beings here as whatever other worldly beings tend to live in your home or visit regularly—goddesses, ancestors, land spirits, nature spirits, and so on. Once you are picking up finer details about your home, eventually, otherworldly beings will (likely)come by and say hello. If other worldly beings aren't your thing, that's okay. Keep working on this exercise, it's still important. If an otherworldly being you don't recognize comes to visit you, always come from a place of respect and deference. Don't make any vows or promises for quite some time. Treat this new otherworldly guest as you would treat a human guest that you would like to impress. Most people would not get married to another human on the second date and most people don't let an acquaintance use their toothbrush. Same kind of sense applies here, *especially* if your troubled times are in part due to impulsiveness. If you're not sure if that applies to you, ask a few trusted friends and family members their opinion on the matter. Once you have all of this down, we can get to building your internal shrine.

When you build and maintain an inner sanctuary, you are building a tiny safe haven for yourself on the astral plane. Kabbala, Gnosticism, and Hermeticism all have some version of this. If you don't have a lot of witchcraft experience, this is a good way to get your feet wet in working with the astral world. Obviously, any time you do magic, there's an element of risk involved. But as previously discussed, every time you get out of bed, there's an element of risk too. Use your common sense and critical thinking skills here, never shut them off while doing magical work. Don't juggle hedgehogs or chainsaws. If you don't feel ready to do this, then you should not do it. Everything is optional, after all.

Your inner sanctuary is a good place to do magical work and to work with spirits and goddesses you already have a good working relationship with. Again, you may not want to invite a first date or new friend immediately into your home, same goes here. You are playing in your own astral internal sandbox, so broadly speaking it's difficult to get too off book here. Treat your inner shrine as you would treat your actual home. You wouldn't invite a bunch of random strangers into your house under most circumstances, nor would you give an acquaintance who doesn't live with you a spare key to your house to come and go as they please—don't do so with your inner shrine. You likely have a general set of rules about how you expect people to act in your home—the same rules apply to your inner sanctuary.

1. If you are not a good visual thinker, this is where Pinterest is your friend. Put together a board for your inner sanctuary. This is where any fussy dollhouse tendencies you may have (or not be aware that you have) can really be their best selves. What do you want the structure of your inner sanctuary to look like? Furnishings? Gardens? Secret passages? Books? Talismans? Do you want food in your inner sanctuary refrigerator (do you *have* a refrigerator)? If you are a good visual thinker or decent as a

visual artist in some way, feel free to build a model or draw a picture and give that part of your brain a chance to flourish.

2. When you are ready to visit your inner sanctuary for the first time, go to a place that makes you feel safe in your actual home. I do a lot of this kind of work either in bed or in my blanket fort, as I live in a small space with Jow and the blanket fort helps me have some (temporary) space that's mine alone. Take some deep breaths until you feel grounded and centered in yourself. If you have a protective amulet or ritual you do for protection, this is a good time to do that. When in doubt, you can never go wrong with a salt circle—so fast, so cheap, so easy to vacuum up.

3. Imagine yourself in a cave. You are holding a torch. You see a set of stairs leading down. Follow the stairs and walk until you see an exit from the cave.

4. When you step outside the cave, what do you see? An ocean, a valley, mountains? Walk until you see a clearing. Wait until you get an omen that it's okay to construct your inner sanctuary there.

5. Construct your inner sanctuary however you see fit, furnish it however you see fit, landscape however you see fit. Make sure it's something you can remember easily, especially if you aren't a visual thinker. The more consistent you can keep your structure, the better a foothold it is for you.

6. When you are done spending time in your shrine, follow the path back to the cave and take the stairs back up. If you had cast a salt circle, clean it up with intention. Resume normal life.

7. Visit your shrine regularly. Make sure it's kept the way you want it to be kept. Change a few small things once in a while—I have roses that grow outside of mine that I enjoy changing from white to pink. Entertain visitors you've pre-vetted. Eat food there, read there, do whatever you like to do in your physical life. The more time you spend in your shrine, the more of a hearthstone it can be for your astral work. It's a good way to develop closer relationships with your goddesses and ancestors because you have a nice place to hostess them. It is also an opportunity to make

the offerings you would want to make there because you aren't constrained by actual financial obligation.

Potential Healing Work for Your Inner Sanctuary

- Crystal grid work, either in your space or on your body in your space.

- Building a bonfire in your inner sanctuary's yard and mediating on aspects of your trouble that you need to let go of and then putting them in the fire.

- Talking to your goddesses and ancestors about your issues and getting their advice (remember, you're not obligated to take their advice!).

- Preparing a healing meal for yourself in your inner sanctuary.

- Taking a cleansing bath in your inner sanctuary.

- Gardening in your inner sanctuary's yard.

- Looking for omens for your next steps in your daily life.

- Magical healing ritual work in your inner sanctuary.

- Whatever you dream up; you're the captain of your ship!

The Moon: A Healing Rite

I suggest that this pair of rituals be done on the dark moon and full moon, but if managing that seems like too much, waning and then waxing are fine. There are lots of resources and apps for where the moon is at your location and time. If you feel called to do this rite on a Tuesday in the incorrect phase, do it. I know some of you want to be purists, but your barn just burned down to the ground. You may as well look at the moon, regardless of her phase. My circle's mantra was "The Goddess is forgiving!" Or, as a friend of my circle once said, "Don't you try to get all high church about this... your circle once had Beltane in July!" (We did.)

In my past life in finance, our mantra was "presentation is everything." It was everything to us because most people couldn't understand the contents of their various packets. What they *could* understand was missing pages, things stapled badly, and so on. While you do need to be able to understand your own rituals, presentation is still important here. We take more care in setting tables for special events. Most rituals should be special, too.

Not every ritual has to be a full tablescaped extravaganza, but consider if you have time to check the internet to find out how to make lavender oil for yourself. Maybe you don't have time to make lavender oil yourself and need to get it at a grocery store, but you *do* have a tiny silver plate to put the lavender oil in from your grandmother, as well as the time to rub some toothpaste on it and use some elbow grease with a microfiber cloth to make it shiny. You know what you can do. The point is to put some thought into your altar aesthetic because it makes the ritual more meaningful.

That said, I've also had days where my altar aesthetic is "I showed up and showered and I think I have all my components. You're welcome." That's a situation where time and effort are the meaningful components because you're probably not doing the dishes that day and dinner probably is going to come from a box. Ideally, at this point, you should be mostly past that stage but showing up and doing the thing counts for a lot more than not showing up and not doing things at all because you are not up to tablescaping.

Later, we'll talk about hexing in case that may be part of your process, but right now you are not clear-headed enough to successfully implement a hex. You may think you are, but you're not. When hexing goes wrong, it's called a mess for a reason. Right now, we're just working on getting your head on straight. You can evaluate if hexing is something you want to do or don't want to do later. Currently, let's keep working through your healing process.

You may want to work on both of the following rituals in the physical sanctuary space you've created for yourself. If that isn't possible because you didn't have the space, outdoors is fine as is anywhere you can be left alone to create your ritual. Make sure your ritual space is tidy, it's easy to get distracted if it's not. If you don't have a mediation cushion, that's also fine. You can use a yoga mat, a blanket, a regular pillow, or whatever is most comfortable for you. You will need a surface to write on, so keep that in mind. I suggest a red pen because red is a fiery color and the color of correction, which is what we're doing here.

Dark Moon Releasing Rite

The objective of this ritual is to evaluate what no longer serves you and to start the process of letting go of these aspects. If you have a different idea on how to get there, feel free to use it instead of this ritual.

Suggested Materials

Rosemary bundle or a bell

Clear quartz crystal

Lavender essential oil

Candle

Matches

Worksheet (Make a photocopy, handwrite your questions and answers in a journal or print the PDF from the (Online) Workshop Community)

Red pen

Meditation cushion (optional)

You can easily create a rosemary bundle by obtaining fresh rosemary at a grocery store or farmer's market. Rosemary is available year round, is not endangered in any way, inexpensive, and is known for its cleansing properties. If you feel called to add other herbs or flowers like lavender or white rose buds, feel free to do so. You will also need some cotton twine. Gather your herbs into a bundle and measure out about a yard of twine. At the bottom of your bundle, wrap the twine around the herbs and tie three knots into it. Then tightly wrap the bundle in the cotton twine up to the top of the herbs and then crisscrossing the twine on the way back down to the bottom of the bundle. Wrap the remaining cord around the bottom and tie a loop to hang the herbs from. Hang the herbs from a hook or a push pin for three days to dry it. If making a bundle isn't possible for you, get a nice bell from a thrift store.

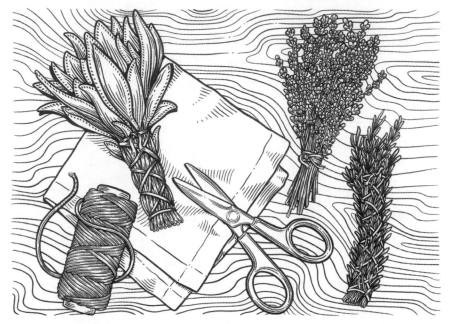

This is how you bundle herbs.

Cleanse your space using your bundle, bell, or whatever method works best for you. Get yourself seated comfortably. Take a few breaths and get yourself centered. Do your best to let go of distractions of the day.

Dab some lavender oil onto your third eye. As you put it on, say, "I anoint myself in the presence of the Moon Herself."

Light the candle. Put a little lavender oil on the candle. Say, "I am ready to let go of that which no longer serves me."

Put a little lavender oil on the crystal. Say, "I am ready to make space for manifestation."

Take your time to fill out the worksheet. The worksheet can be used as a reminder until the full moon to keep clearing space for yourself and to keep yourself focused on healing. When you are done filling out the worksheet, start thinking about what you want to manifest now that there's more space. The universe abhors a vacuum. You want to be the one to decide what to fill this new space with or the universe will get creative. You just did the *solve* part of this internal alchemy, now you need to start preparing for the *coagula* part.

Pass the crystal over the flame of your candle. Put the crystal to your third eye. Focus on what you want to manifest. Put the crystal on your altar or bedside table as a physical reminder of the full moon to come.

Dark Moon Ritual Worksheet

Mediative Questions to Consider	Your Response
What am I holding on to physically that no longer serves me? Why?	
What am I holding on to intellectually that no longer serves me? Why?	
What am I holding on to emotionally that no longer serves me? Why?	
What am I holding on to spiritually that no longer serves me? Why?	
How can I release these aspects to heal?	

Discovery Journal
Write what you have learned from your process here.

Manifestation Notes
Write what you will do to make space to manifest new opportunities for yourself between the dark moon and the full moon.

Interlude Between the Moons:
Cleansing Your House for Manifestation

Make sure you are doing magical upkeep on your house if you want to be able to manifest. If you have wards, regularly make sure they are in good working order. Magical upkeep includes things such as: using Florida water on your doors, mirrors, and window sills; sweeping the energy in your home so it keeps moving; making offerings to your goddesses and spirits; burning incense to keep the energy in your home from becoming stagnant; and so on.

What influences do you want kept mostly outside your home? For me, "negativity" is too broad. I love a good gossipy, shit-talking session, and those are best inside the home. They're also negative AF. If I tried to really banish all negativity, I would eventually wind up banishing myself outside of my own house like a champion. I don't really want that; I pay a lot to live here.

You know what I *don't* like? Slothfulness. I don't like dishes in the sink, clutter, mountains of laundry, piles of recycling, regularly wasting too much time down internet rabbit holes, and not living a reasonably balanced life. For me that includes both drinking a bottle of wine and yelling at the television with Jow *and* not feeling like I'm going to die under a pile of clutter while procrastinating writing this book spending too much time on socials.

I kept trying to banish slothfulness from my house. It would work, for a few days. But it would all start collecting into teeny-tiny energetic dust bunnies (EDBs). After a long consult with Mx. Spice, I realized that the EDBs weren't the problem—I was. Essentially, I kept trying to disassemble them through banishing them and they would just come back bigger and stronger.

I could keep trying to disassemble my EDBs *or* I could name them and put them to work.

EDB are like a pet that can do one thing really well. My EDBs are made up of clutter and slothfulness. They kept reassembling as bigger EDBs. It made sense to put them to work by asking them to gather up all the rest of the clutter/slothful energy by eating it. They are sort of like the sucker fish in my aquarium, cleaning the energy in my home to be more pleasing to me and happy to feel useful.

Start by considering what influences you don't want in your home and if it's feasible to minimize these influences. Picture the energy (I see it as cloudy, dusty crystal shards, but use whatever works for you) in your home or imagine what it feels like. Can you see where this energy tends to collect?

Gather up this energy either through your mind's eye or in an actual basket. Be gentle with it as you will be reshaping it into a new form. Now shape this energy into a small animal. It may not look like an animal we would recognize, and that's okay. Breathe life into your EDB(s) and ask your EDB for their name(s). Mine prosaically are called Flopsy, Mopsy, and Cottontail and look bunny-like. Ask them to eat the unwanted energy in your house. See how it works. It may take time to see results; they are tiny creatures with perhaps more enthusiasm than skill at first.

Remember to thank your EDB(s) for their hard work and to give them some kind of food. You could take some rainbow carrots and leave them out overnight for your EDB(s) and then put them out in the woods for actual wildlife to eat. Think of your EDB(s) more as pet than servitor. They are there to tidy up a little but also to be fun to play with. The more time you work with them, the stronger they will become. Some play could include having them race against each other for fun, petting them within your mind's eye, seeing if they will come when you call them, and introducing them to your inner sanctuary. They are unlikely to topple empires on your command, but we can all use a few sweet small friends in exile.

Full Moon Manifesting Rite

The objective of this ritual is to begin manifesting new aspects you would like to welcome into your life now that you've let go of what no longer serves you. Because the Universe abhors a vacuum, you now need to fill the space you've made with something else. If you have a different idea on how to get there, feel free to use it instead of this ritual.

Suggested List of Materials

Rosemary bundle or bell (the same as used in the dark moon rite is fine)

Rose oil

A candle

Pink Himalayan salt

Your quartz crystal from the dark moon rite

A small pitcher, ewer, or cup

Rose water (store bought or homemade)

Spring water

A large bowl

A good towel

A pen in your manifesting color of choice

Worksheet (Make a photocopy, handwrite your questions and answers in a journal, or print the PDF from the (Online) Workshop Community)

Meditation cushion, yoga mat, or blanket

Cleanse your space using your bundle, bell, or whatever method works best for you. Get yourself seated comfortably. Take a few breaths and get yourself centered. Do your best to let go of distractions of the day.

Dab some rose oil onto your third eye. As you put it on, say, "I anoint myself in the presence of the Moon Herself."

Light the candle. Put a little rose oil on the candle. Say, "I am ready to manifest my set of intentions."

Put a little rose oil on the crystal. Say, "I am ready to receive my intention."

Put the salt and the crystal in the bowl. Say, "I am giving space to be given my intention."

Put the rose water in the pitcher. Fill it the rest of the way with spring water. While pouring the water into the bowl, say, "I open the gate of my spirit to meet my intention." While washing your hands in the water, say, "I purify my hands to accept my intention." Towel off your hands.

Take your time to fill out the worksheet. The worksheet can be used as a reminder until the dark moon to keep manifesting your intention and to keep yourself focused on healing. When you are done filling out the worksheet, start thinking about what you will do to manifest your set of intentions between now and the next dark moon. Look for signs and omens in your dreams, the animals you see, the songs you hear, the words of others, and in your tea leaves.

Full Moon Ritual Worksheet

Mediative Questions	Your Response
What do I want to manifest for myself as I step forward in my healing process? Why?	
What will manifesting this set of intentions bring to my life? Why?	
What fears do I have about manifesting this set of intentions? Why?	
What potential obstacles do I have to overcome in manifesting this set of intentions? Why?	
What can I regularly do to manifest this set of intentions?	

Discovery Journal

Write what you have learned from your process here.

Manifestation Notes

Write what you will do to create opportunities to manifest your set of intentions during the time between the full moon and the next dark moon.

Five
Healing Praxis

The question I ask myself more than anything, during pandemic is "What have I learned?" Some days, the answer feels clear and sharp. Some days, I'm not sure I've learned anything at all. Other days I think I've learned something but when/if the world stabilizes again (or what passes for stabilization), it will slip through my fingers and all of this will have been for nothing. That's the most depressing possibility.

Today, I'm feeling as lucid as my crystal collection, for whatever that may be worth. I think about how I've learned to appreciate the people in my life and make time for them. Tea with MFHG, making my nephew breakfast before school, walking with my sister, inviting my podmates over for anime or the endless walks with them along the shore and forest lines, throwing hatchets for Jow's birthday, having aviation cocktails with Mx. Spice if the weather is good enough, and we're in the same place at the same time, Jow and I yelling at the television together.

I used to be very critical of people chasing peak experiences; I very pompously thought myself different. I wasn't. If there was a fairy-tale monster that did nothing but consume (Vampire? Redcap? Never mind), I was that very thing. I wanted more food, more experiences, more parties, more clothes, more, more, more. I *felt* like I didn't. Or maybe more accurately, I felt entitled to them. I was making the grand sacrifice of working a corporate gig that was slowly crushing my spine and my spirit, after all. Did I not deserve nice things? I worked for them, after all. *Other people* wanted bigger, better, more elaborate parties; bigger, better, more elaborate dining experiences; bigger, better, more elaborate sex things, bigger, better, more elaborate possessions. *I* just wanted a million things from Target, a million brunches and happy hours and a million parties at my house. That was obviously completely different! (Spoiler: It was not, indeed, completely different.)

I've come to redefine what nice things are. Gathering seashells. Cookies shared with me by my nephew. The perfect cup of tea. A lobster in the manager's special case for a lettuce wrap to share with Jow. Wool socks. Sweating into my eyes and my mask during spin class. I worry so much that I'll lose this, if we ever get back to what passes for normal. That I will unhinge my jaw again and instead of consuming these beautiful things I'm graced with, I will instead demand endless amounts of faster food, faster fashion, faster experiences, growing my hungry ghosts until it's all I am, a consuming, consumed thing. I think about this a lot right now during pandemic.

Maybe It's More of a Musical Vibe?

To be truly healed, it is required that you get the cow as white as milk, the cape as red as blood, the hair as yellow as corn, and the slipper as pure as gold. This sounds suitably whimsical and magical, so you're already interested. Now let's substitute a few key phrases so we can figure out how to apply it to your situation. Ready? Okay! The phone calls as long as yarn, sitting in the lawyer's office probating the will until it is spun into gold, the tissues as fragile as ... tissues that are used in your therapist's office, the bills that must be untangled and paid ... are you dying a little inside? It's okay if you are.

As difficult as it is, you have to tend to the practical matters of your troubled times. If it's political upheaval, you need to be writing emails, calling political offices, and joining organizations. If it's the death of a loved one, you have to organize and/or attend services and figure out who is living where and who needs to be fed what and who needs to be separated (someone almost always needs to be separated). If it's career loss, you need to figure out if you can continue in your current field or if you need to retrain in another field and what needs to be done to get there. If it's divorce or a breakup, you need to figure out child-rearing arrangements and financial situations. You see where this is going.

You know what's really hard to do? All the things you need to do when your heart is broken, you're in a fugue state of despair, and your body has turned on you. It feels like running underwater and it's every bit as dissatisfying. Take a deep breath. Let's figure this out. Healing is not going to magically happen for you unless you sort it practically as well, as any of the aunties would attest to.

When writing about magic, I find it most difficult to describe one's will because everyone's will is different. But even if you have a will of steel, it's not going to be super strong right now because you just got repeatedly punched in the face by the Universe. So, for practical purposes, let's just assume everyone's will is garbage right now.

You know what you don't feel like doing when your will is garbage? Listening to other people's problems or going to the gym. You'll have no energy to run down a checklist of soul crushing things that need to be accomplished to dig yourself out of this horrific situation that you likely did not have as much control over as you would have preferred. You'll have to consider if you should perhaps abstain from eating, drinking, and smoking everything that is not nailed down. You'll have to deal with taking care of others, going to the grocery store, going to work (which might be a balm, but maybe not), not spending excessive amounts of money on non-necessities, and showing up for things you have committed to for yourself.

The list is unending, really. This list is as big and wide as your imagination and chock full of things you would rather claw your own eyes out rather than do. But here's the thing. To begin to actually heal, really heal, not social media trash like, "#BLESSED," "#ABOVEGROUND," "#EVERYTHINGISFINE," you'll need to rejoin the land of the living, as my mom would say. And that's hard! You will not want to! It's much easier and much more pleasant to lie on your side on the couch eating Nutella with your hands and watching Hallmark movies. But to actually start moving forward in a real, measurable way, you have to start moving. It's an important part of healing. You could choose to gloss over it, but eventually it will catch up to you and then it will be harder to unravel later. Sadly, once again, the only way out is through.

We like to talk about our will in magic because it's exciting and interesting there. We are summoning dark forces to do our bidding by harnessing our power! We will make our wildest wishes and dreams come true! Then, everyone's interested. Everyone's interest (my own included) noticeably wanes when we are harnessing that energy to make phone calls we don't want to make, when it's about eating food that's actually helpful to our bodies instead of just delicious on our tongues, when it involves getting up at 5:30 a.m. to go to spin class, and then teach our nephew for six hours about concepts that we've mostly shoved aside in our brains to make room for *Real Housewives'* husbands' names (fine, that's my pandemic problem).

But the concept is the same in both places. If you want to be powerful magically, you need to be able to be effective in using your will both magically and mundanely. There are plenty of studies you could check out, if research is your thing, about why delayed gratification helps you develop into a happier more successful person. It doesn't *sound* like it should translate—if you can make yourself trudge through a list of things you need to accomplish to start pulling yourself out of your own personal pit of despair—that you will also be able to do magical rites like the work in this book, but it does. Because they both come from the same place—your will.

In my years of experience with public ritual, I didn't always want to be there either! Sometimes, rituals sounded like a good idea on paper but seemed less good as the day was impending. Sometimes I was busy fighting with other youngs who were helping me make the ritual go. Sometimes I didn't feel well because I have fibromyalgia which gets flared up by stress. Sometimes I had shitty things going on in my personal life—financial problems, sick relatives, fights with significant others. It didn't matter unless it was actually dire. The show had to go on, too many people were expecting a ritual to celebrate a holiday or a full moon or whatever. If I didn't show up, it wouldn't happen and all the work I did leading up to the ritual (because many times, if you were doing it right, the ritual was almost a party to celebrate the months of intensive work leading up to the ritual) would be for nothing. I would be preventing others from celebrating a spiritual event. It's the same thing as if you agreed to head up your kid's classroom book event, or signed on to do a big presentation for work, or if you are a figure skater headed for the Olympic trials. It's the same as if you agreed to throw a party for someone else; you have a responsibility to perform.

In Judaism, it's considered a *mitzvah* to march forward and do a good deed you didn't particularly want to do because it's about the good done, not your feelings or thoughts on the matter. No one cares about your cold, your problems, or frankly, even if you are happy most of the time in this context of obligation. I have done plenty of rituals that could be considered *mitzvahs* where there was very little positive thought or feeling involved, but the ritual happened and most of the time someone(s) benefited from the experience. I have kept plenty of other commitments where the same can be said there too. For many of us, it's easier to keep our obligations to others, but it's just as important to keep these obligations to ourselves. Keeping these obligations to ourselves especially develops our will and makes us stronger as witches and better able to plow through our respective troubled times.

But how? When you are faced with a particularly difficult and arduous obligation that is required of you to move forward in healing yourself, take a deep breath. Remind yourself that you don't have to like it, you just have to do it. Do the thing. As you are doing the thing, reach into your river of sorrow that's within yourself, plunge your hands into it as deeply as you can. Then. Don't. Fall. In. You can scream, you can cry, you can make wordless sounds. Figure out the appropriate physical location for you to be to do this or if perhaps it needs to be internal. Just don't fall into the river. Take that river water through your hands, through your arms, through your shoulders, and you drive that river right down your spine, baby. Do this every time you have to do something difficult and you will find you eventually develop a spine of steel.

Glamour as Healing

When my first husband finally deigned to tell me that he was never, ever (ever ever!) coming back and I was on my own with a mountain of debt with a part time job and poorly medicated fibromyalgia (because that's all that existed then), I wasn't thinking about glamour. My body was turning on me. I was a zombie who could only eat sun-dried tomato Triscuits and bleu cheese if I had two Xanax in me. My then-boss didn't know what to do with me, so she started reading the *Twilight* trilogy to cheer me up ("I don't know why everyone likes him, Deborah! He's really controlling!") and she would bring tiny cupcakes from different cupcake boutiques because that was a thing then. She would also kindly not tell me to perhaps wear something other than black yoga pants and a black T-shirt and maybe consider brushing my hair.

When my uncle died, I wasn't thinking about glamour. I was thinking about my legacy—books and maybe a baby because I missed him so much (I can't explain that particular part of grief math, you'd have to have bio bits that were very interested in having a baby because your baby clock is going off at the same time as your grief clock). I was trying to figure out how to manage this well of grief that resided so deeply inside of me, I couldn't put words to it. I still can't.

When the pandemic happened and I was laid off and Jow was working long hours on the front lines where I wouldn't know when he would come home, I was admittedly thinking about glamour because I had finally learned to start using glamour as a way to cope with hardship. So yes, I was thinking about lipstick, homemade crackers, tiny fancy cocktails, and adorable outfits.

If you recall, you are supposed to be through the initial shock by this chapter, so you are standing on your feet again in a wobbly fawn sort of way. That means you are actually ready for glamour. Most people expect glamour to look a certain way: polished and fierce. But some of my most glamorous moments in life have been in tiny apartments crowded with books and action figures with handmade sausage, St. Germain, extra spindles and roving to use, and a silver lingerie drawer full of Supermoon pastries. Glamour is *also* about being ready to start showing up for yourself and showing yourself that you are worth the effort. Maybe you still feel mostly like garbage, but you're ready to put on scent that makes you feel fierce, or have one special really good piece of chocolate as a treat or to brew a cup of whole leaf tea. When you're ready to start showing up for yourself again in small (glamorous) ways, you're stepping closer to being a little more healed and a little more ready to take on the world.

Glamour is all about showing up and being present in the moment, making the most out of what you have now, which is why it's important in this stage of your healing process. It is not about spending money you don't have. One of my most glam birthdays was the year we were snowed out the evening of the party and everyone put on party dresses with socks and boots to tromp into my house the next afternoon for champagne buckets full of glittering snow and rose petals for big hearty plates of roasted chicken after digging out their cars. It was glamorous because my friends showed up. They had to do actual work to join me. They stuck candles in every macaron, tiny pie, and small cake for me. I didn't need them to bring me bottles of Moet for this to be special and important. I needed them to show up. And they did.

1. **Find the glamour**. Let people show up for you and care for you in whatever ways that are accessible to them. It won't look the way you expect it to but that's what makes it glamorous. Maybe it's eating a delightful cold casserole on your furniture-less floor together, maybe it's walking your dogs outside together in matching tiny sweaters, maybe it's a healing circle with your favorite crystals that they have in your honor, maybe they take you out and feed you full of brunch and mimosas to take your mind off of being sad, maybe they make you little handmade gifts, maybe they binge watch your favorite show with you over Zoom and text, maybe they bring you Clorox wipes (lordess knows that's a pandemic language of love). Let people care for you. It opens more doors which opens more possibilities for magic and stepping forward. You need to be in a place of receiving for you to step forward into your next life here—receptive to new energies, new people looking at your résumé, new dates with new people, new social experiences, new career paths, new places to live, new friends, all of it. Glamour also requires you to be in a place of receiving for it to work, so that's why this dovetails together in your current process.

2. **Fix your skin**. Maybe you're an amazing faerie creature who gets more luminous with hardship (if so, again, please share in the social media groups, how wonderful for you!), but I am not one of those creatures. My body always rewards hardship with delights, such as: a scaly gross scalp, hives, cold sores, eczema everywhere, unexpected zits at over forty, quick weight gain, mysterious ailments that come and go like a sudden aura migraine after never having had them, and let's not forget super fun painful fibromyalgia flare ups because why not me? Skincare is likely the last thing on your mind right now. That's why it needs to be the first thing on your mind. It will also help you re-establish a routine for yourself past occasionally washing your hair and brushing your teeth. Work on a skin routine. I'm talking washing your face and moisturizing. I cannot stress

enough how important moisturizing is. You want to do more? Do more. I also use a toner and a serum. I don't care if you go to a drug store or to Lush or to Sephora or you learn to make your own products from scratch. Taking control of your skin takes control of your own body. You don't have control over all the circumstances of your hardship, but goddamnit, you have agency over your body. Most of us also feel self-conscious (to varying degrees) about our skin being a mess (to varying degrees). Give yourself one less thing to worry about. Make this a new regular habit.

3. **Create a glamour talisman.** It could be a pair of good socks, it could be a pack of sexy underthings, it could be learning to do your hair or facial hair with a specific product, it could be wearing a specific piece of jewelry that you bought during better times, it could be the perfect bag or wallet that you got on clearance, it could be a signature scent, it could be finding the right lipstick, gloss, or balm that makes you feel like a queen. Wearing something that makes you feel glamorous daily gives you back your power which gives you back control over your magic. Put your item on in the morning, make eye contact with yourself for a solid ten seconds in the mirror, gather your will, and say:

> *I breathe, I invite, I knock, I invoke*
> *I gather strength in the mirror manner*
> *Finding my power, I seek to provoke*
> *My cunning to find that I am glamour*

For this small rite to be effective, it must be done every day for forty-two days. If you miss a day, the rite must be restarted from the beginning.

4. **Perform a glamour ritual.** At the end of your forty-two days, seal the rite by performing a small ritual. Put on your glamour talisman and choose your clothing, shoes, hair styling, and cosmetics carefully. Everything is optional in your ritual attire besides your glamour talisman. If you would prefer being skyclad, I would suggest pre-ritual bathing and cleansing, skin exfoliation with a scrub and/or dry brush, and

rubbing body oil on your skin. If you prefer something in between, do what feels right for your ritual attire. Perform the Full Queen of Heaven Vensuian Rite (found on page 85). If you want to add any flourishes, invoke any particular goddesses, ancestors, or spirits; or add any additional ritual work, this is your show, do what you please. After your rite, draw an omen however you like (draw a tarot card, radiomancy, biblomancy, read tea leaves, draw a rune, whatever your thing is), and record the omen and your interpretation. After your rite, a feast that draws in all of your senses is important here. Use your favorite dishes and glassware. As always, don't spend more than you can afford. If you can afford some fresh flowers (or pick some), do. Light some candles, play some music you like. Feel free to invite loved ones or go solo, whatever you like best. Some potential ideas for your feast: roasted beets, a fresh fruit and cheese board, charcuterie, craft cocktails, port wine, iced roasted barley tea, jammy eggs, fresh bread and good butter, smoked duck, rare lamb with roses and pomegranates, rose Turkish delight, dark chocolate. When you have concluded your feast and thrown the last guest out, ceremoniously take off your glamour talisman and put it in a nice vessel or jewelry box. Wear it whenever you need a little extra glamour.

Sometimes You Need a Fancy Dance

This is a more complex work that still incorporates grounding and clearing but should be used once you are starting to feel a little more on solid ground, which is why it's included in the Healing Praxis portion of the book. I've never been much of a ceremonial magician, that's always been more Jow's role in our house. I used to tease him and call it a "fancy dance" because it always seemed to need so much preparation, it required words in other languages, there were specific clothes to wear and as it's colloquially known on Instagram, #ThatBrakebillsShit, which refers to all the crazy hand movements they do to perform magic on *The Magicians*.

It always felt exclusionary, to be completely honest. If we're going to dork out for a moment about *The Magicians* (books or television series, your choice), I always felt much more aligned with the Hedge Witches who sometimes had to do some real gray moral compass acts to shake some knowledge out of the internet or a bored Brakebills graduate. It wasn't a Popper 26 that had been perfectly taught to them by a professional, it was what the Hedges cobbled together for themselves. It wasn't always perfect, it didn't always work well, and sometimes some really gross shit had to be done to get there. *That* always really resonated with me. It's my experience with magic. Not everyone knows eight languages or has an advanced mathematics degree and unlimited funds to access grimoires and ayahuasca retreats. (Too much barf, thank you.)

I wanted to play with a basic ceremonial form and make it accessible. Some witches don't love the idea of making witchcraft more accessible, but secret tradition has never been my thing. The Bible was translated into English in 1526 as the Tyndale Bible, for which a lot of people were killed. I think it's key to keep modernizing witchcraft as well, especially since we're hundreds of years past the Tyndale Bible. Not everything needs to be in Latin to matter. My mom likes Catholic Mass in English much more than she did in Latin; it was a big deal for it to happen over four hundred years after the Tyndale Bible.

America's roots as an immigrant country started over the Puritans' desire to practice their own belief structure, which came about a hundred years after the Tyndale Bible. When we think of Puritans, most of us think about dour people who liked to sue (and occasionally burn) each other. But it was more complicated than that in Salem in 1692. Puritans *also* had teenagers who spent a whole winter roaring like lions in small houses with their parents who were snowed in with them; they wore red petticoats, played games, drank beer, and had a not-at-all insignificant amount of premarital sex. Even the early trials weren't too bad usually, women (especially women of color) were running the show during the early trials for a hot minute. They were taking naps during the day instead of doing tedious chores because they were "possessed" and yes, a few women (usually) were performing a little bit of occasional witchcraft. Mostly things we would now do at sleep over parties. Winters were brutal and boring, what else is there to do? Punishment was basically a slap on the wrist in the early trials, so it was a way to cope with being in a new land with no idea of how anything worked really.

If you have a good ear (and tongue) for languages that are not your mother tongue and you really like doing rituals in Latin and Hebrew (or that's a mother tongue for you), go for it. Love English but it's not your native time? Feel free to go for it. Not based out of the United States and you would prefer your own mother tongue for this rite? Translate away. But for those of us based out of the United States But for the rest of us, there's a strong historical precedence (as outlined above) for performing rituals in your mother tongue, which is why I have chosen to write this ritual in my mother tongue instead of giving you poorly translated Latin or Hebrew as I do not speak either. In reworking this particular ceremonial form, I wanted to make it accessible to those who connect less with "Sky Daddy" energy and more with "Big Mood Queen of Heaven" vibes.

We all need some fancy dancing with the Green Lady to give us a straight shot of glamour during the dark times.

Full Queen of Heaven Vensuian Rite

While you can take this rite apart and rearrange it as you like, doing all parts together one after another is best. In my experience, once you get adept with it, the full rite takes ten to fifteen minutes. The full rite is: Uncrossing Rite to Banish Evil Eye and Other Detritus, Opening the Gate to Your Magical Energy, Rite to Circulate Your Fairy Light Fountain of Glamour, Invocation to the Queen of Heaven to Strengthen Your Magical Power, and Manifestation of Glamour.

Uncrossing Rite to Banish Evil Eye and Other Detritus

This exercise works better standing with shoes off, though it can be done with shoes on and/or sitting. Keep your left hand loose at your side. With your right hand, keep your pointer finger and middle finger raised and your three other fingers curled together. I like to imagine I am clearing my internal aquarium's filter to run nice and clean while I'm doing this, removing dead leaves, dead bugs, and sticks.

Point your right hand at the floor. Say, *Unto.*

Point your right hand to your right shoulder. Say, *The realm.*

Point your right hand to your left shoulder. Say, *Unto greatness.*

Bring both your hands together at your heart's center like you would at the end of a yoga class. Say, *For all that exists.*

Think about your aquarium filter coming to life with a great rush. Put some bass in your voice and say it like you mean it: "In the Name that is above every other Name, I banish all evil influences that have been cast upon me both intentional and unintentional. I cast them out to the black seas of the outer darkness where they will no longer trouble me."

Opening the Gate to Your Magical Energy

Imagine a sparkling glass ball floating above your head. Concentrate on experiencing that ball through whatever senses you work with magically. Imagine turning on the most beautiful fairy lights you can imagine in your glittering ball while saying, "She will be what She will be" three times. Imagine a crown of stars circling above your brow. Open yourself to your goddess self, the part of you connected to the Queen of Heaven.

Spiral your fairy lights from your bright glass ball through your crown and spiral loosely around your head down to your throat. Say three times, "She manifests as a goddess." Imagine a necklace of stars circling around your throat. Open yourself to your talking self, the part of you that connects with intellectual matters.

Continue to spiral your fairy lights from your throat to your heart center. Say three times, "She reveals knowledge." Imagine a brooch of stars circling your heart's center. Open yourself to the deepest part of your heart, the part of you connected with your emotions and the emotions of those around you.

Twist your fairy lights from your heart center to your sacral center. Say three times, "She creates the Universe." Imagine a girdle of stars circling your sacral center. Focus on connecting to the part of you that is creative.

Spiral down further with your fairy lights down to your root center. Say three times, "The Queen of Heaven lives forever." Imagine a star-shaped jewel resting at the base of your spine at your root center. Open yourself to your primal self, the part of you that connects to the world through all forms of desire.

Finally, spiral your fairy lights down to your feet. Say three times, "She is the Queen of the Earth." Imagine anklets of stars encircling your ankles. Open yourself to your earthly self, the part of you that connects with the waking world.

Do not dispel this work yet! You still need it!

Rite to Circulate Your Fairy Light Fountain of Glamour

Bring your attention back to the sparkling glass sphere above your head. Let a gilt stream of light flow down the left side of your body from the sphere. Imagine the left side of yourself being bathed in that light; your shoulder, your arm, your hip, your leg, your toes. When this river of light reaches your toes, start imagining that a river starts flowing up the right side of your body until you reach the top of your head again. Do this three times, breathing deeply and slowly.

Now we're going to add a second circulation, while that first circulation continues. Imagine another river coming from your glass sphere from above your head. This river is going to melt down the front of your body and then circulate back up. Do this three times, breathing deeply and slowly.

Now imagine there's a pool of light at your feet where your circulated fairy-light rivers collect. Breathe this pool of light up through all of the nesting places we've touched on, from your feet to your root to your heart to your throat to your crown. Imagine this light floating above your head and into the glass sphere suspended there. (This is the "whale spout" part some of you may have heard me talk about.) Imagine all this energy spouting through the top of the glass sphere, down your body, and back into the pool of light. Repeat this circulation seven times.

Invocation to the Queen of Heaven
to Strengthen Your Magical Power

"I invoke thee, Queen of Heaven, She who is called by many names and known for her vast unending power. She, whom the spirits fear and love. Hear my call and make all heed my power. Make every spell and scourge of mine obedient unto me."

"I am She, the spirit of sky and star, strong and of immortal fire. I am She, the Truth that calls lightning and thunder. I am She, whose mouth ever blazes. I am She, the initiator and manifestor of the Light and the Dark."

Manifestation of Glamour

Concentrate on what you want your glamour to attract. Think about luxury. Think about what brings you pleasure. Think about flirting with intention with a new or existing partner(s). Think of that fun, flirty exchange where there's *no* intent. *You're so pretty, I'm so pretty! We're both so pretty!* Think about social things that excite you. Think about tiny extravagances. As you think about all of these deliciously glamorous intentions, let your fairy light fountain start to glow a delectable Venusian emerald green. Say six times, "She is the Queen of Splendor. I am Venus's glamour." Seal your intention by kissing your fingertips and offering your kiss to the Queen of Heaven.

Adjust Your Crown Tarot Divination Spread

While divination isn't required after the Full Queen of Heaven Vensuian rite, it's never a bad idea to give a goddess or spirit the opportunity to speak back to you if you spend a lot of time talking to them. Maybe they liked the rite, maybe they didn't, maybe they have some praise to give you, maybe they want to read you to filth. Who knows! The only way to find out is to find omens and get that feedback. Use your most trusted tarot deck for this spread. Focus on addressing what you need to do to adjust your crown while shuffling.

1. What do you need to do to step forward into your new life?

2. What is keeping you in exile?

3. What can your friends and allies do to help you?

4. What can you do to adjust your crown?

5. How do you regain your reign and your power?

Adjust Your Crown Tarot Spread.

Six

Offerings

It's the winter solstice, almost Christmas now. The darkest day of the year. My sister is about to turn forty and has scheduled a mammogram on her birthday because there's not much else to be done safely anyway. She's mad at me about Christmas since I made everyone have an open and honest conversation to figure out if it was wise to all gather. There's too much potential cross contamination for our usual festivities, so it was not. We did not come this far to only come this far. She wanted to hostess and we have never not had Christmas Eve as an extended family in our entire lives, which is why she's mad. We're now ten months into pandemic, it's difficult to do winter without any of the usual small pleasures to endure all the dark days. Nerves are frayed, my own included.

It was an easier decision to come to when we were flush with the news of the new vaccine. Next year would be mostly normal again, we can wait, right? But now we are back to waiting and waiting, trying to figure out who will even be vaccinated when. The vaccine has started to be distributed to hospital staff but not yet to Jow's facility. We wait for the stimulus, we wait for our country to give hazard pay again to front-line workers, we wait for unemployment. A friend of mine got the virus over the holidays and she was frog marched through working from home while "recovering," as we do in a country riddled with a deadly virus. After all, we can work remotely now, so surely we can be expected to never, ever, not need to work for any reason ever. The virus is mutating, the mood of the country is uncertain with the election results, Black Lives continue to matter though fewer people are talking about the importance of the issue as the pandemic drags on.

The vaccine gave a heady moment that maybe there would be some chance of normalcy again, in small, carefully measured steps. I started giddily daydreaming about small things—MFHG over for a weekend, swimming indoors, a happy hour, a gathering of perhaps six whole people. But no one knows, not with mutations, not with vaccine delays. It's Solstice today. My house is strewn with festive natural decorations I've made during moments of optimism. Today, I want to lie on my side in my blanket fort and not get up again. But I keep going to carefully distanced spin classes and writing this book instead. There's some kind of big astrological event today, where we're supposed to work on manifesting our intention through action, especially for air signs (which I am) instead of high-flying rituals. I don't have much of a ritual in me right now, though I appreciate the morning Solstice greetings I received from my people. I keep thinking about darkness and light. I think of Amy from *Little Women,* steering her own ship. It feels too big to steer my ship right now. The swells are too big. My ship is too small. My ship is bound for disaster. Toppled. But still, if we can all wash to shore somehow, I will create my own light in the ruins of this wrecked ship. The tiniest of tealights. The tiniest of sparks. The tiniest of shards of hope.

Why Offerings Can Help Your Troubled Times

I like offerings over sacrifice for this particular journey that we're taking together because it's not about having the luxury to give up baked goodies for the next forty days because you can have freshly sliced mango year round so you don't miss it that much anyway. Offerings can help you out of the privilege Olympics because a gift can be something big (a Peloton bike), or it can be something small (whiskey barrel and hickory smoked salt), much like Oprah's favorite things. It can also be something handmade, carefully found and curated, it can be wildcrafted from the woods, it can be about whatever you are personally good at. Offerings can be an expression of care that requires very little money or financial advantage, which is good because rarely does one have troubled times without financial issues to go with it. Offerings show care to your goddesses *and* they open the door to ask for help and advice.

Whatever your difficulty is currently, having assistance from goddesses who can probably see the board in a different way than we would is likely going to be helpful to move into calmer waters. Goddesses can help you figure out what broken patterns are in your hardship, what you've learned, what you can do differently going forward, and they can offer new solutions to old problems. When making daily offerings, keep a journal or a log of omens you've noticed, new thoughts you're having about your issues, new opportunities being brought to your attention, and old patterns that keep surfacing so you can see the changes that you and your goddesses are bringing to your life together. Prefer not to deal too much with goddesses? I have a water offering ritual to the Universe that doesn't directly work with goddesses or ancestors.

Have You Perhaps Considered Tiny Cakes Instead of Blood?

Let's preface this with the fact that some cultures continue with animal and blood sacrifice today. The practices that have survived this long are often from BiPoC places in the world where colonial imperialism is invested in you wrinkling your nose and saying "gross." I'm sure most of you know this, but for those who don't, in modern practices, the animal is humanely butchered, some of it is offered to the goddesses, and the rest is eaten communally. There's a lot of ritual, care, and thought here. Much more than, say, going to the grocery store and buying a plastic-wrapped piece of meat that has no connection to the animal. If you are part of a community where this is part of your practice, it's just as sacred as anything else. It is equally valid if your beliefs and practices don't include blood/animal sacrifice. If your beliefs and practices don't include this, that's fine too. Onward.

If anything gives me impostor syndrome hives, it's research. I consoled myself in this chapter that it would help us all collectively to know why offerings have been made across the world to goddesses and that I likely knew the research myself, though it was likely dated from ten to twenty years ago, anyway. Keeping up with how our culture changes keeps us plugged in. It's just been a very long time since I was a dewy-eyed, fresh-faced, would-be academic type. With age, I am coming to understand my mother's cranky response to every breakup ever as "irreconcilable differences" because it's what it all boils down to anyway. "Tradition" is her equally annoyed answer to spiritual quandaries, for the curious.

For those who would like a little more, while much of the modern world uses the words "offerings" and "sacrifice" pretty interchangeably, they aren't exactly interchangeable concepts for our purposes. "Offering" means more of a gift and a "sacrifice" is more about giving up something precious. While I do love a good austerity, during a troubled time I can safely say that one of the last things you feel like doing is to voluntarily make your life even harder. I do it anyway in my own practice because it's the fastest way to show the Universe how stone-cold serious you are about something. It gets me into this Inanna at the gate, *who will blink first* staring contest that is incredibly exciting to be part of. This isn't about putting our gender-neutral genital junk on the table right now, per se. If you feel called to incorporate austerity into your current troubled time, I have written about it extensively elsewhere, including my previous book and my blog. If you don't feel called to austerity right now, good news! We're focusing on offerings.

In researching this topic, my favorite thing was how Judaism went from animal sacrifice being part of religious practice to *oh hey, maybe it's much better to try to, like, work on being nice to each other and being charitable to each other rather than such a heavy focus on blood sacrifice. Maybe we would all concentrate better on our day-to-day lives and not be jerks to each other if there was more of a concentration on goodwill. But let's totally put a pin in blood sacrifice for maybe circling back to it later if the Messiah thing works out in future.* Nice for now in Babylonian Talmud times, possibly more blood later. There's some overlap in Hellenic practices while everyone was trying to get on the same page as their neighbors. In Hellenic practices, some goddesses like Aphrodite never cared for the stuff and preferred little perfumed animal figurines instead, and some goddesses eventually opted out of blood and preferred little cakes and myrrh instead. Our tastes change and evolve with age, so it makes sense that the same could be said of many goddesses too. Christianity and Islam, being younger religions, just skipped to the good deeds and charitable donations aspect in offering practices for practitioners. Buddhism, Hinduism, and many Neo-Pagan and Occultist practices stuck with the idea of a gift for a gift. It can be seen as bottom-feeding quid quo pro when you want to dress it down; common hospitality practices when you want to dress it up.

As someone who has hostessed more than her fair share of events, rituals, and parties, hospitality is often underrated. I remember a party where we made sangria and asked everyone to bring wine. Part of what made that party so special is the cocktail and mood of the party would shift as we poured each new bottle of wine into the sangria. It was this beautiful, ever-changing thing. It's important to build communal space together whether it's for a social gathering or a very delicate group ritual, giving others a chance to literally bring something to the table can really help with this. As a hostess, the sexiest thing you can say to me is, "What should I bring?" I like it when people bring flowers or a bottle of wine, but I also like being asked. Sometimes I need ice or toilet paper or garbage bags or diet tonic water. Sometimes it's something vague like "a protein" or "something non-alcoholic to drink." On the off-chance it needs to be said—if it's anything more than the most casual get together with you and a friend and cups of tea—bring something. Always, always. What also counts? Doing dishes, taking out the trash, helping your hostess if she gets cornered by a guest by starting a conversation with that guest so she can keep circulating, arranging plates, and so on.

It's not like the goddesses are any different. Sure, they will understand an occasional extenuating circumstance where you have shown up empty handed and asking for lordess knows what and then bouncing without so much as refilling an ice cube tray. But generally? They are going to give you the stink eye just as much as I would at a party. No one likes freeloading. They are also much more likely to be kindly inclined to listen to your petitions and aid you in some way if you make the effort to show that it's appreciated. If I needed to borrow money from my mother (or some other person I have a close relationship with), a half dozen cannoli are not going to be an equally reciprocal gift. But I know she likes cannoli. I know I can afford cannoli. I know cannoli will make her feel like I appreciate what she's helping me with.

I also shouldn't show up to my mother's (or other close person) only with my hand out or waiting to load her down with every problem ever without reciprocating. I should show I appreciate her when I don't need anything. That means all kinds of arcane things, like helping her take Christmas decorations down from the attic, going to the pool with her because it makes her happy, going to a Zumba class even though I hate Zumba with a passion, drinking the white wine she likes when I'm with her, taking her out for breakfast, calling her even though the phone is the Worst and we live super close to each other but she likes the phone, traveling with her and building memories with her that way. Same thing with your goddesses, though they will likely want other social exchanges.

Much like in human relationships, you should have a consistent back-and-forth with your goddesses. I paid for coffee this time, she drove to the beach. I listened to two and a half hours of (gender neutral) boy problems, he helped me shovel my car out of the snow. I invited them over for a home-cooked meal and they brought a dozen good macarons I like. It's not going to always be equally equal— in general, that's a miserable way to live. But it should be equitable.

The equation gets tricky because it's cooking, emotional labor, time, money, and handmade goods. But you know when you feel resentful in a relationship because you have to do all the heavy lifting and you know when it feels like both of you are pulling the cart. If you are giving a goddess offering after offering after offering and all you're getting in return is radio silence, I'm sorry to say but she's not that into you. Even if you do have a really good conscientious relationship with your goddesses, it's not always going to be an easy solution to all of your problems through goddess intervention. They are busy, they have problems of their own, and they have their own lives. But maybe they will pop a nice piece of cake in the Manager's Special case after a really crummy day, which is better than nothing by a lot. Unless you don't eat cake. Then, hopefully, it's cheese, fancy bread, or a fresh pomegranate in the case, or whatever.

Offerings and Cultural Appropriation

This is obviously a delicate subject. My moral compass may be set differently than yours. Maybe for you, you only feel right doing Nordic rituals because that's your lineage. That's fine. As someone who was adopted, I don't really enjoy bloodlines and DNA the way a lot of other witches do. Hereditary witchcraft really does not do it for me. It's okay if it does it for you. You will be the only person who knows what feels morally good or bad for you, so you will need to use your own judgment on that issue.

My personal line in the sand when it comes to my spiritual practice is that I feel okay working with any goddess who seems interested in working with me and using any general population ritual format. Using Catholicism as an example because that's what I grew up with, anyone can attend Mass. Anyone can light a candle for their Mary of choice. You are not supposed to receive communion unless you are Catholic and have received that sacrament, same with confession. If I was not born Catholic and had not received my sacraments, my personal rubric/moral compass would determine that it's fine to go to Christmas Mass and light a candle for my preferred Mary. I would not feel comfortable with receiving communion or confession without having previously received those rites.

I've never personally been terribly interested in initiatory practice past my Catholic roots. I don't tend to trust other people enough for it. I also have never been terribly interested in collecting occult merit badges. It's become very fashionable in occult circles to be a specialist in something. If that's your passion, by all means. Find a reputable teacher, do your research, get to know the community, find out what is considered culturally appropriative, and why. Make sure to find out how to be respectful in learning your new practice, figure out how you fit, and how your magic works within those circles. Live your best life.

In any situation, don't just do something because you read it in a book. Figure out if it's actually for you and why. Always work with goddesses you have a pre-existing relationship with first—they are going to be much more invested in you. There's nothing wrong with occasionally making new goddess friends, but you also want to develop actual meaningful relationships with them. If something doesn't feel right or feels disrespectful for you to do spiritually, don't do it. It's that simple.

Offering Disposal

I'm often asked how to dispose of offerings. There's a lot of fancy, more traditionally correct answers to that question. Burying them at this or that phase of the moon, leaving them at a crossroad at midnight, releasing them out to sea, leaving them in a forest. As a modern witch, while not the biggest eco-warrior the planet has to offer by any stretch, I have come to prefer to not leave out any offerings that could harm the planet or local wildlife as much as possible. If you really want to dispose of offerings traditionally, you should only offer food that won't hurt animals, biodegradable paper, soy or beeswax chime candles with cotton wicks, fresh spring water, coreless incense (Japanese incense is good for this), and flowers.

That said, sometimes I need to give perfume or food that isn't animal friendly. A small portion of your offerings may be kept for altar décor (things like jewelry or animal horn). But your altar will get out of hand fast if you keep everything, which makes it difficult to continue to make new offerings. In those situations, I do my best to recycle what I can (glass jars or bottles, tin cans) and I pour the liquid offerings down the drain of my (preferably clean) kitchen sink. I toss out the food in the garbage. If you have a compost heap, feel free to compost whatever can be (eggshells, coffee grounds, etc.). If I know the spirit or goddess well enough, I may pass the offering forward if they want me to (gifting the perfume to someone, etc.).

Generally speaking, I let things sit out for one night so all of the spirits and goddesses can get their fill. Don't leave out anything overnight that pets or children could get into unsupervised that could harm them. Put it out of reach. I have never had an issue with any goddess or spirit being offended by my practices of disposal. Occasionally, one will want a few extra days with their offering(s), but that's about it. Small space living and concerns about local habitat are both far from new to goddesses when it comes to human concerns.

General Offering Practices

Goddesses usually have specific offering preferences that are well known within their pantheon (and the internet). They will also have specific offerings that will be made known to you specifically. I have a teeny tiny Ganesha, about half the size of my thumb. The tradition is for him to be made of water soluble clay and then you melt him in water because he was made for a specific holiday. But I (unwillingly) fell in love with him and wanted to keep him. Our arrangement is that he particularly likes giant offerings (for the size of his statue) from me—apricots, plums, mandarins, lavender shortbread cookies stacked as tall as he is, marzipan fruit, towers of kaju barfi, rose Turkish delight—basically whatever filters through my kitchen that he's interested in and is the correct size. He has now upgraded to living inside a tiny halved coconut, a metal crown, and being hand fed little marzipan fruit.

Finding offerings that are specifically between you and your goddess takes time, attention, and a deeper relationship, much like with people. You will notice a friend likes seltzer pretty quickly, but it will take longer to know that her favorite food ever is a leftover beef marrow bone with day-old Yorkshire pudding.

But rejoice that there is a goddess equivalent to seltzer. It is typically difficult to offend any spirit, goddess, or ancestor with offerings of fresh spring water, incense, and tealights. If you are asking your goddesses for help with your difficulties, larger offerings are never a sad thing. That said, it's hard to ignore persistence. Fresh spring water, incense, and tealights are inexpensive enough if you go to the right places such that you could make this offering daily to all of your goddesses. Remember: goddesses often have different agendas, moral compasses, and world views than many humans do. While the help offered may be easy to recognize and what you would hope to receive, it may also seem like a bigger immediate mess and more problems. Yes, you could ask for a specific, tightly-worded intention. But then you also assume that you know exactly what would fix your problems, and it takes out the opportunity to find new solutions and options that you never would have thought about yourself. It's like going to a friend for advice but only being willing to act on the answer you want to hear. Your friend is going to be annoyed and lose interest in helping you. Goddesses aren't often that different in that regard. Set your intention for what you need, but leave some space for your goddesses to do their work. Be a squeaky wheel and check in daily with your goddesses while remembering to thank them for their time and anything you've seen done.

Pretty Committee President (and Demon Slayer): Durga's Origin Story

While Durga is incredibly fierce, she's also a Great Mother figure. She will try to resolve issues first with charm and softness, but if the issues will not be resolved with soft skills, she's not afraid to be as brave and savage as her lion, Gdon. She understands how to solve problems creatively and can also be very soothing and kind to work with, making her an excellent companion during arduous points in your life. One of the oldest ride-or-die goddesses, having her on your side while you smooth out your life will make the process easier.

Shiva was hanging out in the cremation grounds with his buddies when he noticed a buffalo demon creating an extraordinary amount of devotional energy for him.

"Hey," said Shiva. "Great job, my man."

"Thanks!" said the buffalo demon. "I've been working really hard on it."

Shiva nodded thoughtfully, exhaling on some really choice cannabis. "Yeah, so. I should give you something. What do you want, bro?"

"To be immortal!" the demon said immediately.

Shiva started to grant his petition and then laughed. "Nah, you got to die, dude. It's the rule."

The demon thought for a long time. "What if I could only be killed by a woman? How about that?"

"Done!" Shiva said quickly. "Enjoy it, demon guy!"

He wandered off in a cloud of smoke to consider universal secrets with his entourage trailing behind him.

The demon immediately went to work, gathering up all his little demon friends and immediately destroying the mortal world. Once that's wrecked, he starts thrashing out in the heavens until all the gods and goddesses are forced out.

"Shiva," said Vishnu sternly, once he tracked him down. "You need to fix this."

"Chill, chill, chill," Shiva said brightly.

"I will not chill," Brahma said tensely.

"All we have to do is make a bad-ass beautiful, charming, smart goddess who can destroy demons. So, a goddess like my wife, Parvati. But she'll need more demon-slaying powers."

The three gods immediately got to work creating the goddess as well as copies of their weapons for her to wield, calling her Durga (दुर्गा), meaning "invincible one." Himavan was impressed so he gave her a lion for her to ride, so she could be even more fierce.

Durga immediately started raising her own army, creating warriors out of her own breath. She got the mortal world back under control, so the demons sent word to the buffalo demon that she was coming for him. She was unstoppable and the most beautiful being that they had ever seen. The buffalo demon wasn't too concerned. What could a woman do?

When he saw her, he was immediately taken with how gorgeous and graceful she was. He turned himself into a handsome suitor and knelt before her, asking her to marry him. Since Durga was also very cunning, she immediately knew it was the buffalo demon she had been sent to kill. She arranged her hands prettily in the proper mudra.

"I would be honored to marry you," she said sweetly. "But I am not permitted to marry anyone unless I can be defeated in battle."

He laughed heartily. "Then we shall be married very quickly!"

She narrowed her eyes and hissed, "Come at me, bro."

The battle raged for days and days as Durga defeated his troops with her army. When it finally came time for the buffalo demon to fight Durga, he changed forms many times, hoping to confuse and outwit her. He turned into a lion, into an elephant, and finally into his buffalo form, charging directly at Durga. She never wavered as he came upon her, and she neatly took his head off completely with one stroke of her sword. He was defeated, causing a beautiful fragrance of flowers to pour from the sky. She closed her eyes, regaining her breath as all of the rest of the gods and goddesses thanked her profusely, planning festivals in her honor.

About Ganesha

In both puja practices in this book, you will always need to honor Ganesha first. In Hinduism, the edges get a bit blurry. While each goddess has her own form, preferences, and skill set, she *also* tends to overlap with almost every other goddess in some way. Durga, for example, can be considered a form of Parvati. Kali is considered an aspect of Durga, with her base form still as Parvarti. Ganesha can be considered the child of Parvati, Durga, Kali, and even Lakshmi.

It can be argued that Ganesha has two mommies (Parvati and the Earth Mother make him together in Parvati's bath while Shiva's off contemplating deep truths). His brother, Kartikaya, can be argued to have two daddies (Agni and Shiva make him while Shiva's off in the woods with Agni doing who knows what) though they are raised by Shiva (who is considered to be father to both Kartikaya and Ganesha) and Parvati (who is also considered mother to both god children). I love these stories because even thousands of years ago, blended families existed and many of Shiva and Parvati's stories of marriage are about fighting, laughing, fucking, and saving the world. Much like his dad, Ganesha is a really chill dude until he's not. If you put an obstacle in his way, he will trample it to the ground, just like an elephant would.

From a puja perspective, it also makes sense to start with Ganesha because he's an elephant-headed god who is the remover of obstacles. You want your work in your puja practice to go smoothly, starting with removing anything that might be preventing you from obtaining your petitions. There is also a mythological reason we start with Ganesha.

Ganesha has a brother named Kartikaya. Kartikaya is a bit of a jock/warrior type. He always wants to go rock climbing and be active, bouncing off the walls and generally annoying Ganesha. Ganesha usually just wants to listen to records, read obscure comics, eat a ton of sweets, write on his hidden blog, and have his brother leave him alone.

One morning, Kartikaya was outside Ganesha's door chanting his name until he finally opened the door.

"What?" said Ganesha.

"Brah, let's do something!" Kartikaya said, bouncing on his heels.

"Pass," said Ganesha, starting to close the door.

"Come *on*. You never want to do anything."

Ganesha sighs. "Why? What do you want to do?"

"Race! Let's race!"

Ganesha stared at his brother and thought for a long moment. "Okay, fine. We'll race. But only under one condition. Mom and Dad decide who wins."

"Deal!" exclaimed Kartikaya, already zooming off on his peacock.

Ganesha felt a wave of relief wash over him. He knew he'd have days and days to himself without his brother bothering him for once. He could do whatever he wanted. After a while, once it felt like enough time for Kartikaya to have run it off, he came to breakfast with his parents. He crumbled his idli into smaller pieces while he considered what to dip it into. His parents were laughing and squabbling as usual over cups of masala chai.

He cleared his throat and said obsequiously, "Mummy, Daddy?"

They turned and looked at him expectantly.

"You may have noticed that Kartikaya has been gone for a while."

As he suspected, they had just realized this now. He schooled himself not to roll his eyes. "He wanted to do a race with me," he said, just a little petulantly. "And I said okay, but only if you both would decide who the winner is."

His parents exchanged a look. "But why are you at breakfast then?" his mother said finally. "You know your mouse is much slower than his peacock."

"Yes, that's unwise," his father agreed.

"I couldn't bear to be away from you," he said, with just the right amount of drama he knew they both secretly loved. He slowly and carefully got up and circled his parents three times, bowing to them. "*You* are my world. And now I've been around you three times!"

His parents were still laughing just as Kartikaya came through the door, his chest puffed up almost as much as his peacock's. "Well? I won, right?"

"We have to give it to your brother," they said, explaining what he did. Ganesha shot his brother a look of triumph. Kartikaya rolled his eyes and mouthed *suck up* as he went to go find his cleats to go play soccer with his friends.

And this is why in puja practice, Ganesha is always acknowledged first.

About Agni

Most deities are gods or goddesses of something: goddess of the hearth, goddess of happy marriage, goddess of prosperity, and so on. Agni isn't the god of fire, he *is* fire. There is a distinction there. In Hinduism, whenever you light a match, a fireplace, or a bonfire, you are invoking him. He is also considered the mouth of the goddesses. So when you light your ghee lamp in puja, it's important to acknowledge him because he's the mouth/gate your goddess will speak through. If you can't get your ghee lamp lit, the puja can't move forward, your offerings can't be made, and your petitions can't be heard, which is why it's important to always say a few words of praise for him when lighting your lamp.

Puja Offerings to Durga

I spent a lot of time learning how to perform puja rites from patient Indian puja supply shopkeepers and various aunties. For those of you who are reading me for the first time, this is the puja I've used for the last two decades; so far, I have not had rocks thrown at me by angry goddesses. I'm not an expert in Hinduism, I am simply a very enthusiastic devotee to a few goddesses there. If you want to give this a try, you can get supplies at a local Indian store and support local business. If you don't have much of a local Indian population, you can search online for a Hindu puja supply shop you like or from Etsy or Amazon; whatever is best for you. Many of the supplies you may be able to make yourself. For internet searching purposes, *puja* is also sometimes spelled *pooja*, so try both when in doubt.

You will need:

- Two small fireproof bowls

- Two potholders

- A picture of Durga that you have either bought or printed out from the Internet, ideally in an inexpensive frame.

- Kumkum powder (you can make this yourself potentially, search "DIY kumkum powder" on the internet)

- 1 T Ghee (you can make this yourself potentially, search "DIY Indian Ghee" on the Internet)

- A bell that's dedicated to Puja Rituals

- Sweets (search online for "Sooji Ka Halwa Recipe" if you want to be fancy about it. If you have a local Indian bakery, she'll be happy with anything there. Packaged Indian sweets from a Desi market are generally well received as well, as is dried fruit in my experience. I personally have found Durga to be fairly open to sweets in general, especially if it's coconut flavored, like a fresh macaroon.)

- A small plate for the sweets (read about *prasad* in the ritual instructions)

- Cotton wick (search online: "how to make a cotton wick for puja")

- ½ of one camphor tablet

- Small cup (e.g., a shot glass)

- Good quality milk (you will learn more about why in Lakshmi's puja on page 141)

- A lighter

- Fresh, brightly-colored flowers, such as mums or chrysanthemums, plus a vase
- Incense (I find she's partial to jasmine) and incense burner
- Tiny picture of Ganesha in a frame
- Smaller amount of sweets for Ganesha, in front of his picture
- Mala beads

Durga Puja Set-Up

1. Before starting, set up your altar area with Durga and Ganesha's pictures. Put the fireproof containers on the pot holders. Put the ghee in one of the containers, and soak the entire wick in ghee. Put the camphor in the second container. Make sure your lighter works. Arrange your sweets on the plates. Put Durga's sweets in front of her picture. Put Ganesha's sweets in front of his picture along with a couple flowers. Pour the milk into the shot glass. Put the incense in the burner. Arrange

your flowers. Put all of that in front of Durga's picture. Arrange the bell, the kumkum powder, and your mala beads in your set-up.

2. Starting by facing the picture of Durga. Turn in a circle clockwise, clapping your hands eight times for the eight directions as you turn.

3. Ring the bell. Announce the date and time and your intention (e.g., "I am here to perform a puja for Durga.").

4. Acknowledge first Ganesha for being awesome and removing the obstacles. He always is thanked first before any actual puja activity starts because of the race he won against his brother; his parents decided that's how things should be going forward, as previously discussed.

5. Light the wick. When lighting it, thank Agni for being there as fire and acting as a gate. Light the incense. Light the camphor.

6. Tell Durga about the sweets, milk, flowers, and incense you got her. Show all of these things to her by holding them up to her picture's eye level. In your own words, tell her how awesome she is. Tell her why you want to work with her. Ask for her help. Say her seed mantra: *Om Hrim Dum Durgayei Namaha* (Ohm Ha-REEM Dum Durguy-yay Nahmah-hah). "Salutations to the goddess who protects me!" You can look the mantra up on the internet if you're not sure about pronunciation. It's not required but it's good brownie points to say her mantra 108 times, using the mala to keep count.

7. Put some kumkum powder on the picture, on her head and feet. Then take a little off the picture and put it in your hair or on top of your head. Kumkum powder stains, so be careful.

8. Thank Ganesha for his presence. Thank Agni for his presence. Thank Durga for her presence.

9. Ring the bell.

10. Clap your hands in a circle clockwise in all eight directions. Say, "This puja has ended but I welcome your company if you want to stay."

11. *Very important:* You *must* eat some of the food you gave Durga or she will think you gave her garbage, an incredible offense to Hindu deities.

This practice is called *prasad.* If you give flowers, some flowers must be given to others. If you gave sweets, eat some of them. It's also encouraged to share these offerings with other people as well, to share the experience of being in Durga's presence.

Offerings to Yemaya

In the beginning, there was a great god of the sea. He was lonely because the sea was empty. No tiny fish swam in great schools, no fearsome crabs with great claws, no tricksy octopuses to cleverly hide and escape, no deep sea monsters to fear, nothing. But the god of the sea was friends with another god who would want to wash in the god's ocean. The god of the sea said that his friend could not wash in the ocean for it was too deep and he would drown. The ocean god *would,* however, make the ocean accessible if his friend would start creating life. Life of all kinds. So his friend created crabs and kraken, birds and beasts, bees and buttercups. Soon Yemaya was created, and from her womb came the other orishas. She loved her human people as much as the orishas who came from her own body. But while everything was being created, there needed to be something more to keep things interesting—some tension. Some drama.

Some evil.

It wasn't long before many of her human people were being stolen from her, crammed together in the holds of ships to be taken to new lands and enslaved. The sound of the Mother's wails were so great and so fierce that they reverberated across the ocean's floor. She followed her human children to their new lands through the sea, comforting them in their new places.

Her sister, Oshun, was never too far behind her. She was the orisha of the rivers, flowing out to her sister. Oshun knew how to get a man heated. She loved nothing more than the gifts they would bring her, the way they would kiss her neck, the feeling of having them inside her, the compliments that they couldn't stop themselves from giving her. And if she became pregnant, well, these things happened. She knew she could rely on her sister to care for her children, flowing from her river into her sister's ocean working together harmoniously. Most of the time. (Sisters.)

Yemaya as a fierce mother goddess is perfect to work with during your difficulties. She can firmly help you get back on track while offering nurturing vibes. With that in mind, the odds of having problems, reading this book, and New Year's all happening at the same time are rather slim. It's Yemaya's traditional feast day as well as when her devotees make wishes and offerings for the new year. But much like you won't be too sad getting an off-season pumpkin spice latté or a piece of gingerbread in the summer, a gift is still a gift and a wish is still a wish. If it *does* line up like that for you, you should make sure to get to the beach on the right day because clearly it was meant to be. Don't have a beach? That's okay, a river will work too. If you use a river for your offerings to Yemaya, you should offer praise for her sister, Oshun, and bring a little something for sis. Oshun likes peacock feathers, high-grade honey, pumpkin, and sunflowers, among other things.

To make a melon boat offering for Yemaya, pick out the loveliest, freshest, juiciest melon at the grocery store. Cut it in half. If it is a melon, such as a cantaloupe or honeydew, scoop out the seeds. It will create a natural cup shaped indentation. You will want to arrange seven white flowers, such as roses, around the indentation. Write out your wish and fold the paper toward you and put it in the indentation. Put a small candle in the indentation on top of your intention. Keeping the environment in mind, take off the metal from a tealight or use natural wax candles made from beeswax or soy. Don't worry if it doesn't light or stay lit, it's usually pretty windy on the beach. It's not really an omen in my experience generally. You can also offer a small, fancy white-colored sweet (or a good piece of pound cake) and perhaps a small bottle of rum (you can pour it into the water and recycle the bottle). When you get to the beach, give some words of praise to Yemaya and concentrate on your intention. The omen you are looking for is for your melon boat to go out to sea on the first wave, not immediately to wash up to shore. Nothing terrible will happen if that happens, it just may mean that your wishes aren't fated for the year or that they will be harder to achieve that year. But that is not to say anything about the following year. That said, you can wade out a bit and try to judge the waves. It's a bigger sacrifice in colder climates during the winter and it's never a sure thing but more effort is almost always universally appreciated.

Offering Melon Boat

Water Offerings to the Universe

Maybe you don't want specific relationships with goddesses, spirits, and ancestors for whatever reason. That's completely fine, I see you too. Maybe you prefer to think about the Universe that resides inside you instead of the cosmos, that would also work here. Maybe you are giving your goddesses offerings but also need to do something to calm and focus yourself during this time of upheaval. Maybe you are someone who finds comfort in looking for the Universe's patterns and threads and how they work with your patterns and threads.

While Buddhism is a smaller part of my background, I have adapted this practice that I have found lovely from a Buddhist practice. In Buddhism, this is an offering to the Three Jewels: the teacher, the teachings, and the community. The teacher here is the Universe, the teachings are the ones the Universe gives us daily, and the third is your own community in whatever way you see it—it could be your extended family, your friends, your polycule, your coven, your social community (like the SCA, Girl Scout parents, a convention or festival you attend, your AA home group, etc.) or some combination thereof. You can do this either as a meditation or with eight small physical bowls or cups, such as ramekins or sake cups. You can also do this as an internal meditation, whichever you would prefer. This would be a good thing to do to start your day with, in the morning. Start by making sure the bowls are clean to represent a fresh start to the day. Start with each bowl upside down on your altar (you can also use your inner sanctuary as part of this if you are doing this as a meditation) or it's like you are offering the Universe as your guest an empty bowl instead of something refreshing. Turn your first bowl over and fill it with fresh water, preferably spring water or distilled water. As you're pouring, consider your moral compass and how it aligns for you. This is an offering to the Universe. Turn your second bowl over and fill it almost all the way up with the water from the first bowl, leaving a little water in the first bowl. As you pour, consider your relationship with food and how you would like to be nourished with food. This is an offering to the Universe. Turn your third bowl over and fill it with the water from the second bowl, leaving a little water in the second bowl. As you pour, consider your relationship with your body and how you can nurture your body. This is an offering to the Universe. Turn your fourth bowl over and fill it with the water from the third bowl, leaving a little water in the third bowl. As you pour, consider your relationship with yourself and how you can be gentle to yourself. This is an offering to the Universe. Turn your fifth bowl over and fill it with the water from the fourth bowl, leaving a little water in the fourth bowl. As you pour, consider your relationship with your brain and how you can care for your brain. This is an offering to the Universe. Turn your sixth bowl over and fill it with the water from the fifth bowl, leaving a little water in the fifth bowl. As you pour, consider your current distress and how you can move forward in your life. This is an offering to the Universe. Turn your seventh bowl over and fill it with the water from the sixth bowl, leaving a little water in the sixth bowl. As you pour, consider your relationship with your spirit and how you can sustain your spirit. This is an offering to the Universe. Turn your eighth bowl over and fill it with the water from the seventh bowl, leaving a little water in the seventh bowl. As you pour, consider your relationship with your voice and how you can use it to create change for yourself. This is an offering to the Universe. Namaste (the divine in you recognizes the divine in the Universe). Now, working right to left, pour the water through the bowls until all of the water is back in the first bowl. Pour the water into a small offering vessel. Turn the eight bowls upside down again to dry. Leave the first bowl of water out overnight as an offering and then the next morning use the water to water indoor or outdoor plants and turn that bowl upside down as well to dry and begin the offering again.

Seven
Ancestors

Your actual dead people will be full of complications because they aren't mythic; they are people you used to fight with. They are people you may have had difficult relationships with. They may have had questionable politics and other really irritating things about them. If you are like me and don't insist on shining up your dead so they were just beacons of virtue, you will remember these things in great detail. You are not obligated to make offerings to any dead who caused you trauma. You're not obligated to anything, really. If you want visceral ancestor relationships, this is where the sausage is made. You can ignore it; you don't have to pick up every shiny thing ever. It might not be for you if you can't stand any of your dead people. It happens.

Hoodoo talks about a cemetery being alive when the spirits that reside there are live. That's great when you're doing the kind of work that requires active dead people. When you are visiting your dead people because it's what your mother would want you to do and said dead people would want you to do, live to me means that descendants are actually participating in ancestral rites. A great graveyard environment should have people planting trees all over the damn place, Pop-Pop over there has a boss train set up on the little shelf of his tombstone, someone baked cookies into wreaths over here because I guess Aunt Hilda was really into that, it looks like mini-actual-Christmas at the dead kid's grave a row over and has for forty-one years. Maybe it's like the one time I almost got locked in the cemetery one Christmas Eve because there was a lot of traffic and my mother was really determined but not nearly as determined as the dude who was string-ing lights on an actual six-foot tree at dusk as we sped out as the cemetery staff was closing the gates. I don't know what the other dude's plan was. Hopping the fence? Friends with Cemetery Dude? No idea. But these are a bunch of really, really motivated descendants. And I'm 110 percent into it. Let's discuss what this rite actually looks like. Not the idealized version, but the actual ver-sion. You will just have to take my word for it because I suggested interviewing MamaFran for this project and she bellowed, "It's just common sense, Debbie!" Which I took to mean that she's uninterested in your education, even though I pointed out if you haven't had a parent dragging you to dead people hangouts all your life, you may be a bit spotty on protocol.

You may have cremated dead people or dead people who are buried too far away to visit. No worries, just use the mytho-poetic version. If you have dead people in the ground, you aren't mad at them presently and they are within rea-sonable traveling distance? Saddle up!

You may not know where your dead people are currently. That's okay too. You probably know someone who does. You could start by searching "finding a grave"; there will be websites such as FindAGrave and BillionGraves to start. If you don't have any luck there, you would need to join a site like Ancestry.com and allow that site to have your information and possibly pay a fee to find your dead people. If you can get the name of the cemetery, it gets much easier to find your dead people. Most cemeteries have books or computers with everyone's locations. Once you find your people at the cemetery, it can be helpful to drop a pin on Google Maps to make it easier to find them next time. Helpful items to bring to your cemetery jaunt are: a small shovel, scissors, pruning shears, a cou-ple bottles of water, a couple flower cones, twine, ribbon, fence stakes, a garden-ing kneeling pad, a couple rags, a soft tooth brush, and an offering. Your offer-ing will likely depend on what your family's traditions usually are. Some people bring grave blankets, some people bring real flowers, some people bring pretend flowers, some people bring food, some people bring coins, some people burn incense, some people bring trinkets that they think their dead people would have liked, some people bring stones, some people bring things that your dead person liked in life like a favorite newspaper or coffee.

The very first thing you do is check out the neighborhood. Are there a lot of offerings out? That tends to cheer the place up. It also gives you an idea of your cemetery's culture. Next, you need to get your dead people's spots in order. You may need to plant something, you may need to use ribbon to add festive ornaments to your dead people's headstones, you may need to practice gently kicking over your dead husband's log/greenery arrangement to make sure it's heavy enough to withstand the heavy wind that happens there while clutching curling ribbon so you can somehow tie it to a flat stone (... possibly just MamaFran there). This is why you brought your gardening cushion, so you can really get in there. We often do rock gardens, mostly to keep us busy as small children but we still do it currently. This requires a lot of rearranging, finding new rocks, and keeping the border tidy. You will need to weed and also give the headstone itself a good scrub, possibly also washing it down with water using your rags and soft toothbrush. Water and prune any plants. Plant anything you intended to plant. Make sure your offerings are secured to the spot in some way, whether it's using stakes in the ground or tying the offering around the headstone. If you are an apprentice to an elder of some kind in this expedition as I am, your main job is to troubleshoot her problems, tie ribbons, weed, crouch down to get at things, rearrange the rock garden, water the plants, and admire your elder's work. Basically, the same job you've had as long as you can remember. This *sounds* easy, but the weather is often freezing, raining, or generally miserable.

Here is where media teaches you to give a long soliloquy to your dead people. That has never happened in my experience, though yours may be different. If it's a nice day, you might have a little light chat that's approved by your elder. If you want deep feels talk, you better be prepared to drive out there solo on your own time. Especially if she's feeling antsy. If she's feeling antsy, good luck getting more than a Hail Mary and two signs of the cross. Silently.

The actual dead people site work takes maybe ten minutes, but isn't that most rituals? If you do just the actual work part? For me, ritual prep is so much more to do with it than the actual ritual work. That's been the case for as long as I've been in charge of rituals. In this particular rite are the car rides of indeterminable length (and enduring them), discussing why what my mother's offering is tops, doing the cemetery part, having Sicilian pizza by St. Charles at my dad's, and then going to the Italian market two doors down where my mother can contemplate never having to cook ever again and I can buy inexpensive prosciutto and lemon ricotta (another pro for my favored cemetery—incentive to go). By my dad's, we examined a greenhouse full of poinsettias including hot pink that neither of us could buy due to pets but enjoyed taking in. Sometimes we talk about memories in the car. Sometimes we sing along to the radio. Sometimes we gossip. Sometimes we ignore each other. Sometimes we get on each other's nerves.

The format is simple—say a prayer of some kind, leave an offering of some kind, take care of the land that your deads' bones are nourishing, say another prayer, do something life affirming. Sometimes, simple is where everything happens in between the threads.

Offerings at Home to Your Ancestors (The Mytho-Poetic Version)

Some of us have complicated relationships with our actual dead people. I have a complicated relationship with my bloodline ancestors because I didn't actually know any of them in the present. I have a complicated relationship with some of my more recently deceased for an exciting array of various reasons. That said, it can be helpful to have ancestors to call upon in your magical work. Much like with goddesses, you will need to spend time developing a relationship with yours and you should not only call them when you need something. It annoyed GamGam in life, it's going to annoy her in the afterlife, too. Your ancestors (chosen or blood related) will generally be interested in your success because of their personal connection to you either through blood or through your relationship together. Again, when you are at a low point in your life, having all the help you can get will move you forward. Your cemeteries may not be super close to get to, mine are all over an hour away so visiting often isn't really an option. It's important to me that my deceased show up also at my house. I'm currently working on clicker training my still-living mother that while I will go to the boring-ass cemetery she has insisted on to be buried in a few times a year, the real party will be at my house. Cannoli live at my house. Showing up to my house equals cannoli.

This year, with the pandemic, I've had a lot of questions asked about the recently deceased as there's been more unexpected deaths than usual. The first question I always ask the (living) grieving, is "Do you want this dead person to live with you?" It's okay to say no; you might not be ready for that level of commitment with that dead person. You may still have issues that you're still working out about that person or that person's death. If that's the case, you're not going to banish them or dispel their spirit. That's crazy. This is a person you care about, even if it's complicated. You're not going to murder a friend for overstaying their welcome on your couch, it's the same thing here. Do you have friends or family in common? Maybe one of them would like your recently deceased to reside with them. You can also ask your recently deceased person if there's someone else they would like to stay with and offer to make that connection for them. If you feel the spirit of this person showing up in your home and you're not ready for it, just keep gently reminding them that you are working through everything too, and Friend said it was okay for the deceased to stay with them.

If you decide you want to hostess your recently deceased, their spirit will likely be strongest in the weeks following their death. It can help to set up their new place of residence as soon as possible to get them settled in. If your deceased are less recent, you can still follow this suggestion, it just may take longer for them to show up. It's also not uncommon for a more recently deceased person to show up regularly and then show up less regularly. You can also use this to get in touch with ancestors you never knew, if that's your goal. Ancestors from centuries before you came on the scene can be excellent support because they may be interested in you just because they like the cut of your jib. They may be curious to see what you can accomplish since you know how to read, generally have enough food, shelter, and fresh water; and you have interesting technology and the same laugh as their sister did. You can also invite chosen ancestors. You don't need to be blood-related; you can invite deceased friends or make new (deceased) friends. Just remember that much like in this world, spirits sometimes misrepresent themselves to become friends with you. You'll need to figure out criteria for making new spirit friends and vetting them.

Start by setting up a picture of your deceased (if you have one) or a representation of the deceased you are inviting. If possible, pick a permanent place and plan accordingly. You can lay down a little altar cloth and put out a little plate and cup along with perhaps an incense burner, if you like. It doesn't have to be really complicated. If that's too much space, go back to the Altoids tin altar model but with your ancestors in mind. You can do an internet search for ideas for that. If you have any relics of your ancestor (a lock of hair, a ring, a diary, a small object that was once theirs, etc.), add that to the shrine. You can offer them water, light, and incense, much as you would your goddesses, especially if you're not sure what they liked in life. And remember, spirits will often ask for things they enjoyed in life but you are under no obligation to give it to them. For example, my ancestors will receive cigarettes over my cold dead body. That said, I'm often asked to have coffee, candy, a nibble of a seasonal treat that looks good, a shot of whiskey, and so on. Generally speaking, you don't share offerings directly with your ancestors. If you made a cake and gave the first piece of cake to an ancestor, you could eat the rest of the cake but would not eat that piece. If you receive specific instruction from your ancestor to do otherwise (many of my more recent ancestors don't like food waste), follow your intuition on that. My uncle often asks Jow to share his treat with him and there haven't been any ill effects from it.

Keep in mind while you're building your practice that the more often you make offerings, the more often your ancestors will hang out in your house. Were your ancestors bossy and pushy in life? Guess what—they will still be in death! You are ultimately captain of your own ship. If your ancestors are giving advice that you feel goes against your best interest, don't take it. There's nothing my recent ancestors would love more than if I had at least three kids. My current living ancestors are a bit sparse in children, so *someone* should clearly pick up the slack. Babies will fix everything! Except I live in a tiny space with fibromyalgia, and I'm over forty. So … not so much over here. Much like living with any relative, either you both come to terms with each other (they want me to have babies and I'm not doing that) or you can't. We've come to terms with it more or less over here, so they don't really press the issue. Also, being over forty to them means I may as well be a hundred and forty in terms of baby making; they've conceded the battle there.

Figure out how strong a presence you want your ancestors to have in your home. More offerings will make their presence more strongly felt in your home, and fewer offerings will make their presence less strongly felt in your home. Too few offerings and they won't show up. It's a delicate balance. My uncle's presence is fairly strong here, though he comes and goes and does what he pleases, much as he did in life. But we're pretty ideal for each other—he was often a cheerful bachelor in life who liked nice things, loved to travel, didn't much care about neatness, appreciated creativity, was childless for much of his life, liked... romance (let's go with that), food, and new experiences. Think about those aspects before you get your cousin with terrible views on gender and world cooking to be hanging around your place 24-7.

Mary, Untier of Knots

If magical dead people (saints) aren't your thing, they don't have to be. Having been raised Catholic, saints are one of my favorite parts of Catholicism: they're weird, they were once mortal, many of them are a lot more lax about you being a witch as well as whatever iffy personal habits you may have, and they did intense devotionals for miracles/magic. If your practice does not line up with working with saints, that's fine too.

Mary has a lot of different names and faces to her. Mary, Untier of Knots has become more popular due to Pope Francis (hands down, favorite Pope for me). I like that her novena is super new and fresh and I like that she's all about day-to-day problems and getting them straightened out. She's only been revered since the 1980s, so in terms of church-speak, a hot minute. Her first painting showed up in the 1700s, by Johann Georg Melchior Schmidtner. Mary's chilling out on a crescent moon with angels, stars, and doves, as usual. Her hands are busily unknotting a ribbon, while homegirl's foot is firmly planted on a snake's head, just in case he was considering getting away while she's working on her knotted ribbon. She is the picture of, "Don't worry, I've got this." All the tribulations that have brought you to this point in your life can be untied, unknotted. She is particularly helpful for addiction, anxiety, and family and marriage problems, but this is also a Mary who gets the everyday grind of all of the small problems coming together to wear you all the way down. Her feast day is September 28. If your problems and reading this book line up for that, great. If not, that's okay too. Rarely is anyone sad about getting gifts when it's not their birthday or a holiday.

If you are someone who likes physical representations in your magical work, you can simply print out a little picture of her painting, light a tea light in her name, and use a long cord. Using a long cord, put a knot in it, naming each problem as it comes to you. Ask for her help in your own words as you unknot each knot.

If you would like a prayer to go with that, here is a simple prayer I have written:

Our Lady

Undoer of Knots

She who understands

She who loves the lost

She who has unending

strength and compassion

With your powerful hands

Guide me to untie

[insert your issues]

Mother, hear my pleas

Mother, intercede on my behalf

Mother, help me free myself

Amen.

If you are someone who likes something a bit more fancy, you can always research her novena which goes on for nine days with a different meditation for each day.

Eight
Protection

On New Year's Eve, I went to the spa for the hot tubs with NurseCat. I wanted to do a fancier, bigger version of that last year, but I was stuck at home, sick as a dog. The hot tubs here only kind of worked and they were having issues with the water. The saunas were closed. It felt like the right end to 2020. Good intentions, lukewarm hot tubs. For the first time since I was a kid, I didn't stay up, I went to bed with Jow who had work the next day. I went to an early morning yoga class, I couldn't figure out where it was being held so I was late. Everyone had perfectly toned yoga bodies and added extra more difficult poses effortlessly to their flows. I fiddled on my mat and tried to stay engaged. Mostly I felt frizzy and uncoordinated, my flows ever hindered. After, A1 came over to make melon boats with me for Yemaya. We wrote our intention papers, we drove out to the shore. I waded out and my boat was swallowed whole but not before I was soaked in sea water. We played with a new app that was supposed to take you somewhere interesting. It kept taking us back to the ocean and eventually the closed Convention Hall in Asbury Park. I thought about how much time I spent over the summer walking the boards there, the concerts I had seen there years ago with beautiful boys banging on upright pianos covered in punk rock stickers. We had all been so young then. I still felt hopeful, then. I was feeling shades of that hope, even as I programmed my mom's Apple watch for her, quizzing her on its functions and breathing down her neck about how to call for help in an emergency as she once did with me when I was a child. We got to the Breathe function and I explained how it worked. I could tell she thought it was bullshit. But

I explained it's supposed to lower her heart rate. We sat quietly and breathed together, intentionally. It was the first time, and likely the only time, we would share space together like that, with her grandfather clock ticking in the background. I felt close to her in a way that was hard to explain in that moment. She checked her heart rate. Much lower.

The vaccines were rolling forward, Jow had been scheduled for his first dose. It would look good in Georgia during the special election only a few days later. Maybe next summer I'd drink frosé outside the Convention Hall and eat a plate full of oysters. Maybe there'd be live music again next summer. Maybe I'd get to have six people over for a dinner party. Maybe, maybe. I registered for my vaccine, I had a group number for it.

And then there was a coup.

It's really difficult to write and work during a coup. Watching our country's capital get its windows smashed out, the current president cooing about how they were all good people. He wasn't saying that during the BLM protests. Then it was nothing but law enforcement armed to the teeth and tear gas. Because this is what democracy looks like right now in this country.

I kept writing anyway. I worry as I write that I talk too much about myself, that I'm talking too much about this moment in time. But I also think about how important it is to have some voices of our people on the record about this. The witches, the occultists, the heathens, the druids, the dabblers.

Me, Jow, and John (my writing partner) are holed up together as the coup unfolded. John and I had been friends half my life, he is in psychiatric healthcare as well as a stand-up comedian. When he came over, he said, "Do you guys know a coup is happening in Washington?" We didn't, we had all our media off because I was writing. While I felt sick and I was breaking into hives (predictably), John was holding up remarkably well given that he's Black and there were plenty of bullets and tear gas for peaceful BLM protests but practically a red carpet invitation to raid our nation's capitol. The boys try to get Wi-Fi working, talk about the nature of evil, and eat donuts. John tries to distract me by attempting to start feuds about if Hot Pockets and Pop Tarts are ravioli as he edits part of my book. Jow gamely replies and talks about pastry crust and how it's different from pasta dough and they settle on classifying them as pies. I'm trying to think about protection magic. If I was the witch I'm supposed to be,

I'd be doing it right now to protect the capitol. But I'm a deer in the headlights, terrified about what's going to happen. We don't even light candles. We sit not far from my altar. I wonder if that's enough of a talisman for a coup? I don't even know any coup protection spells. John tries to deescalate the coup with words. It's both our best powers anyway. We call it a tacky coup and embellish on news stories, on how the people involved with the coup are doing it wrong. We make jokes, we talk about psychology and their mommies and daddies. We hope that if we keep telling the story in the right angle, it will twist the threads of the story enough that we can go to bed not scared out of our minds.

The day before, I was telling John about my research for my book. How twenty years ago, there was barely a book available about BiPoC goddesses. I told him about the year Katrina happened and we floated melon boats out to sea in New Jersey, in January. It was so cold. There were refugees from New Orleans who knew what we were doing. They asked for boats. We gave them ours. Now, doing additional research, I can look to Black (cis) women talking about these goddesses on YouTube, telling the goddesses' stories. I see Beyoncé and her sister Solange, dressed as beautifully as Oshun and Yemaya; Beyoncé talking about the goddesses in her lyrics.

For a moment, I feel so fucking happy that the world is here, in this place.

And then I think about Katrina (I still think about Katrina all the time) and how our country let an entire gorgeous city be swept out to sea with so many people killed in it, I think about Breonna who was asleep in her bed, I think about Trayvon who was just walking, Atatiana who was home with her nephew, Stephon who was in his grandmother's backyard, and how the list goes on and on. All these unarmed Black people who were just trying to live their lives. I think about how many Black people have been killed until I feel so sick I cry and feel like throwing up (I still think about them all the time). I think about this ridiculous and awful coup, how many people would be shot on sight if they were BiPoC, how the streets would be washed in blood if that was the situation instead of cops who were sworn to protect democracy standing around while the capitol got ransacked. I feel really sick again, watching this. Watching offices be pillaged while our elected officials hide, terrified they'll never see their families again. It's just so much to take it.

I was once a nanny, so I also think about *The Cat in the Hat* and how that cat wrecked that house down to pieces and everyone was worried that the mess was too big to fix. There's a few pages of hand-wringing about it and Mom and Dad coming home and knowing that you let a random sentient cat into the house and let him wreck the place. But because it's Dr. Seuss, the cat comes back with his boss cleaning machine and everything is okay again. Mom and Dad don't know you had a massive momentary lapse in judgment, the cat that made a mess cleaned it up, and everything has been reset back to normal.

But the cat hasn't come back. Not here. And I don't know when he will. I don't know if he will. I don't know if we've finally made such a big mess that we can't go back to our country's normal settings, not with the cat, god knows where, doing god knows what, showing no sign or interest in fixing it. It scares the hell out of me that he won't ever come back. He won't ever fix it.

Shielding

Most occultists/witches have really elaborate shielding systems. Real talk here: I can't be bothered. Jow has compared this to constantly eating an egg salad sandwich out of a bus station bathroom vending machine, a la *Futurama*. It totally squicks out every magical person I know. Just the idea of all of that foreign flora and fauna blossoming into strange inner terrarium creatures inside me sends a shudder down their collective spines.

The thing is when you're used to a stream of low-level junk coming through your energetic system like leaves or bugs through a pool's filter, you tend to notice when it's a dead bird and not a leaf. Like, say, the evil eye.

The evil eye is a good example of a low-level *malefica* that most people will have to deal with. Social media doesn't help this. Most of us use social media to project an idealized version of our lives and leave the tedium of the day-to-day. Even though (hopefully?) most of us know that social media is used this way, we still tend to see it as an unvarnished look into someone else's life instead of the polished version that it is. In this modern life, if it's not pandemic (when it is, we can't see each other much anyway) we're so busy running from one obligation to another that we don't see our friends in person as often as we once did. We see their Best Party Selves on social media. We start to think that this is exactly who this person is, forgetting that everyone has problems, bad days and things they aren't talking about publicly. Most people don't often take pictures of the awful parts of their day, many people don't talk about their deepest personal struggles on social media (and almost no one talks about unresolved issues publicly), so all there is to go by are the best parts. If you're not having a great day, you may find yourself feeling angry and/or jealous about others because we're thinking about our shitty day and all our problems and all the things we're not sharing on social media. This leads to the evil eye because we're either purposefully flinging some spiteful energy at that person or telling ourselves that we're happy for them while subconsciously flinging hateful energy. Fun fact, magical *and* nonmagical people can throw the evil eye. Non-magical people are often *better* at it because it's all subconscious and unintentional.

So, how do you know that someone is giving you the evil eye?

- Sometimes you feel it. I feel it like a dart to my back, right where my bra strap hooks. It usually comes to your back. When you feel it, yank it out. I usually use a literal yanking motion to take it out. It physically hurts me. It's never a bad idea to wear a protection charm either around your bra (if you wear them) or on a long chain that drapes over your back.

- Are you involved in frenemy warfare? I spoke about frenemies in my last book and why they're bad to have in your life. Lots of things that are bad for you taste delicious. Frenemy warfare can be occasionally productive if you limit it to holding up the traits you admire about the other person (which is ironically why you're mad and jealous). Acknowledge that you're jealous of it, be mad that you don't have it, then figure out how to use that energy to make yourself faster, smarter, stronger. Few of us have that kind of self-control though. Most of the time it degenerates to *OMFG I hate that bitch! Who does he think he is? She is not better than me. I am better than them! I want to tear their face off!* Then you're too consumed with the toxic energy that you are generating and too busy getting yourself trapped in a revenge cycle to use it productively. Be honest with yourself and where you are with it. You are giving that person the evil eye and that person is giving you the evil eye right back. You're both erecting giant shrines to each other because you're so consumed with each other. The only way to fix that is to fix yourself by disengaging. Admit what you admire, work to bring it into your life. Then, let it go. Let. It. Go.

- Are you projecting an image of perfection? Don't be a target. Be sure to "let slip" some imperfect aspects of your life sometimes on social media. If people see you more as a whole person instead of a Ms. Martha (Stewart) level of perfection, they are less likely to target you with their negative energy. Because let's be honest. We all liked Martha more after her prison bid.

- Are you attending an event that has a high "woo" ratio? It's not always just at "Occult/Pagan" events. Lots of alterna events including conventions, kinky events, and renaissance fairs have a lot of witchy folks there. You get a lot of us in a room and one of two things happen: either the preexisting issues between any two or more witches boil over into a mess of woo/crazy/evil eye/intentional hexing, or having all of us in one place together when we *don't* already know each other and *don't* know how to combine our collective energies makes a weird oogie-boogie egregore. Things will get weird and gross because … welcome to being magic.

This is where you need to be especially defensive, even more so than in your day-to-day. Wear a scarf over your head to protect your crown chakra; if it's outside wear sunglasses (your eyes are the windows to your soul, but don't wear sunglasses inside unless you need to for medical reasons). Limit direct eye contact, wear protective jewelry, draw protective sigils on yourself using hand sanitizer, ask for your goddesses' and spirits' protection, and consider wearing gloves if you can. Try to pull all of this off in a way that doesn't look obvious or awkward.

Now you can recognize the evil eye and defend yourself. There's also another option in dealing with this kind of thing. Don't be afraid to shove that energy right back at the person who gave it to you. You could feel it as an energy push inside yourself, you could hold a mirror up to their picture (or to the actual person if you can be slick about it) or you could picture handing that person the ball of energy they slimed onto you. Just because it may have been subconscious doesn't mean you have to accept that negative energy or be nice about it.

Regular cleansing is also important to make sure your magical filter doesn't get clogged too much. Ideally, at least once a week. You wouldn't go months without physically bathing; you shouldn't go months without cleansing.

You can perform the Full Queen of Heaven Vensuian rite, you could smoke yourself with sacred herbs, you could take a bath with cleansing herbs, you could take a shower with a salt scrub and visualize the negative energy going down the drain, you could also go to a sauna and sweat out the negativity. Self-awareness is the most important aspect, however. You know when you're about to get a cold. Your head feels stuffy, you're sneezing, you're sniffling, you're coughing, and you feel run down. You should be able to tell when your filters are getting clogged, too. I feel more run down, less energetic, more depressed, more tired, and disinterested in things that usually interest me. When I feel like that, I start by cleansing to see if it's a filter issue or a depression issue. If I cleanse and I feel better for several days, it's a filter issue. If I cleanse and don't feel better, it's a depression issue that I need to address through my depression coping routine.

Be gentle with yourself and let yourself learn and grow in your own way. Eventually, it will be like second nature. Be sure to trust your instincts if something (or someone) doesn't feel right to you. It's better to politely (or not so politely) back away and find you were wrong, than to have not backed away and found that you were right and in a bad situation.

Stay Inside the Salt Circle

If you are having nightmares due to your arduous current moment in life, you can always lay a salt circle around your bed. Salt circles are awesome in media because they always look really austere against a hardwood floor. The reality there (as someone who has tried) is that you would have to pile your salt really high and use some kind of small brush to keep it neat. You would probably need some kind of way to make sure your circumference was perfect too. It sounds like a hellish job for some poor PA on set. While you *can* do that for yourself if you have that kind of time and energy, you really don't need to. You can get salt that you like (I like sea salt personally, but some people prefer

Kosher) and then inscribe the box or canister with protective words and symbols in Sharpie. You can set this salt aside from your food salt, on your bedside table. Before bed, sprinkle salt around your bed. In a firm and commanding voice, tell the nightmares to leave your bedroom. You can picture them as black horses, running out the bedroom door, on their way to greener pastures. Keep setting the circle at night until the nightmares stop. The best part of this is that it's easy to sweep or vacuum up.

The warding process that I will be discussing has its roots in hoodoo practices. I am not initiated into the tradition, but its basic spell work does not require that. Hoodoo tends to be regionally influenced in practice and often will have bits of local immigration practice involved in it, such as in the Pennsylvania Dutch Pow Wow, but it is predominately a Black tradition. Traditional hoodoo often uses Biblical verse as it's often used in conjunction with Christianity. I have found some alternatives because while I do enjoy working with saints a great deal and also adore certain books in the Bible, it's not comfortable for me to use verses that are traditionally used because it's not where my power is. If your power is there, feel free to do research on which Bible verses are used and why.

Use a physical broom to sweep unwanted energy from your house, making sure to get inside closets and to do the entire house. Sweep it outside a door. Seal your mirrors, doors, and window sills with rose water, Florida water, or holy water (whatever your personal preference). You can draw protective words and sigils into this work. Get four small cups like shot glasses. Put a dime at the bottom of each one. Cover each dime with dirt that's from your property as close to your house or apartment building as possible. Sprinkle some Florida water (you can buy it at a botanica either in person or online. I've bought mine from a regular grocery store before. I was surprised to find it in the hair care aisle, though I shouldn't have been. It's one of Florida water's traditional uses) on top while reciting the following:

> *Yet this is my comfort: when your words are done,*
>
> *My woes end likewise with the evening sun*
>
> William Shakespeare, *The Comedy of Errors Act 1, scene i*

Place each shot glass into the four corners of your home, preferably in places where they will not be knocked over by children, animals, or visitors. I keep one corner of mine in a cabinet for that reason. As you place each glass down, imagine roots sprouting from the dirt growing through the foundation of your house into the deep rich soil of the land where the roots can grow strong and weave a web of protection through your house.

Fuck Right Off

If you are worried about your safety due to a bitter divorce or breakup, bad blood with someone due to your current difficulties, or a particularly angry family member or friend, you need a little more than basic shielding. First, get a restraining order and make sure you keep any evidence you might need for the future, such as emails, texts, social media posts, and so on. You will likely want to consult a lawyer about how to proceed in this situation. Use common sense, look into resources about what to do in this situation. Magically speaking, while this isn't exactly hexing, it's also not "positive vibes only." You will need to figure out if your moral compass allows for you to take proactive action against this person. Your goal in this work is to get this person away from you, ideally at least a hundred miles away from you. The focus is that you feel safe and protected in your home, not to hex this person.

The following work is based in Hoodoo, so you will need a personal effect belonging to the person in question: (ideally) hair, spit, sexual fluids, or blood that came from this person. Used toothbrushes, socks, underwear, and hairbrushes are perfect. Rub the petition paper against a personal effect to "transfer" it to the petition paper. If you cannot get those things, you will need a photograph. In this digital age, there should be no reason you can't get a photo.

Get a large piece of a brown paper bag. Write out why you want to have this person be a hundred miles away from you. If you are feeling (somewhat) benevolent, you can add things like "for the job they've always wanted" or "for an amazing love interest" or "for a beautiful house"—whatever you think would get them gone. While writing the petition, you want your pen to never leave the page. If it does, start over.

Petition Paper Example

Put the effect on the paper. Put poppy seeds, black salt (you can make it using iron filings or ash; there are plenty of recipes on the internet), and red pepper on top of the effect. Fold the paper seven times away from you (the "away" part is important here). Drip a black chime candle over the paper to seal it shut. Speak with conviction about why it would be great for this person to be at least one hundred miles away from you. Put this working in a zip-top bag and take it outside where you can find it.

This next part is the most challenging: ideally you timed your working to be the night before what follows as you will likely need most of a day for this. Grab your working. Mix some salt, lemon, and hyssop into a spring water bottle that is ¾ full with spring water. Take that too. Drive or take public transportation to some place at least a hundred miles away from you (that's about two hours each way by car). Find a dumpster. Take your working out of the zip-top bag. Toss the bag. Speak over your working again about why this person needs to be at least this far away from you. Toss it into the dumpster. Wash your hands with the spring water mixture. Walk away, don't look back. Return home.

St. Guinefort Does a Protect

St. Guinefort is one of my favorite saints of all time. The myth goes that a bunch of people in France in the Middle Ages were having all kinds of fantastic results from a new saint, St. Guinefort. A shrine had been built for him and he had been saving women and children during childbirth, saving babies, saving people from dying of plague. So the Vatican is like, "this seems pretty dope, let's send one of our dudes over to certify St. G's miracles and get him added to our rolodex." The Vatican sends over Stephen of Bourbon to see what's going on. He sees the shrine and all the offerings, he hears locals recounting how awesome St. G is. There's just one small thing: St. Guinefort is a dog.

The Tale of St. Guinefort
St. Guinefort was a good
doggie who lived near Lyons
in France
When his master left to
go hunting,
St. Guinefort protected
his master's child from
a snake by killing the
bad snake
When his master returned
and saw St. Guinefort
covered in blood and
did not see his child,
he killed poor St. Guinefort
The master then saw his child
and the dead snake
Feeling terrible that he killed
his best and most trusted friend,
he buried St. Guinefort with all
the honors a doggie saint deserves
Many people visit St. Guinefort's shrine

to ask for protection of their children
and bring flowers and treats
because you can't keep a good doggie down.

The Vatican beat a hasty retreat and tried to futilely remind people for the next eight hundred years that dogs "can't" be saints. Needless to say, it never stuck.

Prayer to St. Guinefort

Our dear St. Guinefort
Protector from plagues
He who loves unconditionally
He who cares for the defenseless
He who has unending
kindness and devotion
With your strong heart
Please protect
[name anyone who needs protection, including yourself]
St. Guinefort, hear my pleas
St. Guinefort, intercede on my behalf
St. Guinefort, please protect myself and my loved ones
Amen

Suggested Offerings for St. Guinefort: Fancy doggie biscuits (especially those that can be shared with local doggie friends or donated to a local shelter), a white vigil candle, Evian water (St. Guinefort *is* French after all), the most delicious of the table scraps (anything but chocolate). You can share the fresh water with your house pets and/or leave out some water and treats for neighborhood pets/nature spirits.

Nine
Lucre

There's a part of pandemic that no one likes to talk about. It's not the hard parts about how NurseCat and Jow became friends because they have literally moved bodies together or about the refrigerator trucks outside of hospitals or morgues that became too full for more bodies to be added to them and how there needed to be ad hoc procedures for temporary storage of these overflow dead people. I mean, yes, all of that is terrible and why Jow has pandemic-related post-traumatic stress disorder.

But also? In the earlier days of pandemic, for the first time in our lives, for a hot minute Jow and I were filthy with money. Now, we've always had more than some (two cars, enough food to eat, the ability to afford medication, a condo that we own) but also significantly less than others (we don't have a house in the Hamptons, we never got bottle service at a club when that was a thing, no Rolex watches, we have just one bathroom, no one has a Tesla, no one gets filler in their faces here).

I learned very quickly what I would do with twice as much money as we used to make (though we all knew it would be temporary). I could walk into a grocery store and buy whatever I felt like: fresh figs, new loose teas to try, smoked duck, fresh cut pineapple, fussy little pastries, whatever I wanted. I had never had that experience in my life before, more than anything that made me feel like we were rich. We had a cushion in savings in an amount we had never even been close to. We were able to diversify our portfolio a little. We paid off some credit cards. I got yoga leggings I had always wanted and silver Birkenstocks. Jow got good

133

quality scrubs and new books. We were able to donate to small businesses and charities we cared about and got takeout from our favorite restaurants to support them. We got subscriptions to media that we cared about.

It was really exciting that if we had small problems during this time that our friend Money could solve them for us. Money had previously been a fair weather and often unreliable friend, though we had come to a point in our lives that we could usually pin Money down enough to make sure Money showed up to pay all necessities. Often, we could force Money to commit to being there when we needed Money to be there. On occasion, Money would grudgingly manifest in our house so we could go on vacation or have a night out. But now? Money was suddenly ride or die for us and ready and willing to help solve any issue that Money could solve.

The pandemic forced us to really consider what was worth spending money on and what wasn't. It wasn't as if we were previously completely dedicated and committed on our side of the fence to money, either. I had a Target habit and was an ardent brunch hound; Jow loved Starbucks, expensive small press books, and takeout whenever possible. Pandemic started in earnest while it was too cold to eat outside. Takeout was great when it was something we would be too lazy to make at home, like really good Indian food or truffle ramen or paella. But for brunch, it didn't make sense. We could just make it at home. When we could eat outside again, we quickly learned that brunch only made sense under very specific circumstances. For us, those circumstances were when it involved empanadas or cocktails that we wouldn't be motivated ourselves to make. Otherwise, it felt like a waste of money.

In some ways, there are fewer ways to spend money during pandemic (restricted travel, no happy hours, no concerts, less impulse buying). But in many, many other ways, it was just as easy to blow through money like water. There's now delivery of everything to your door, curbside pickup for everything else, you are suddenly sick of some of your household goods and cannot stand to look at them any longer. I have started to hate our older damaged wall-to-wall carpet with a great devotion, much greater than a vague occasional dislike when I thought about it in pre-pandemic life. It's the same with your closet because who knows what to wear anymore anyway, and now your home is your office, your kid(s)' school, your gym, your spa, and your bar which requires shifting and new containers, so many new containers. In our household, we quickly saw that attempting to manage our finances as two separate entities while Jow was working all the time was not going to work. Together, we decided that I would take over our household finances so I could patch up any financial leaks and make sure everything continued to be paid on time, which has worked for us for the last six months.

Beautiful Dirty Rich

Obviously, as you can hopefully ascertain from the previous section, I'm not a financial expert. At all. That said, because I haven't always managed my financial life correctly, I do know how to attempt to shake some money loose from the Universe. It's typically not going to be an exciting amount of money in my experience, but it will usually cover what you need it to cover.

I've also learned in my years as a Witch that if you don't ask for something, you're probably not going to get it. If you live somewhere where you can generally have Wi-Fi, a mostly full tummy, clean water, and medical care, you already have more than most of the world. While that's definitely worth considering in any kind of gratitude work you may do for yourself, it also doesn't mean you have to be completely and utterly satisfied with what you have currently because of that fact. The whole point of magic is to be brave enough to ask for more.

We can wring our hands all day about "deserve." Do I deserve a fulfilling relationship? (Yes.). Do I deserve to not be forever punished for my hardships even if I played a role in them? (Yes.). Do I deserve to live in a country where everyone's right to love who they want, to have autonomy over their own bodies and physical safety while going about daily life are guaranteed? (Yes.). Do I deserve to feel pleased with my imperfect body? (Yes). Do I deserve to have a career that doesn't grind me down? (Yes.). Do I deserve prosperity? (Yes.) But "do I deserve" is not actually the question; it's never a matter of "deserve." If it was, privilege in modern society wouldn't be a problem because anyone who had any power would completely and unequivocally deserve it. I don't know about you, but I can think of several people just off the top of my head who probably don't deserve what they have. We don't do witchcraft to be given our tiny appropriate portion of what we deserve, we do it to get what we actually want. If you want more money, ask for it. If you want much more money, ask for it. If you want a vault of money to swim in, ask for it. It doesn't mean you're guaranteed to get it, but nothing in life is a promise. People die, things break, tragedy happens, that's what brought us here. We can weep, wail, and gnash our teeth, or we can do something (like magic) to actively make change in our lives. Yes, obviously, you should also look at your budget, look at your investing, look at your bad financial habits, look at your current career, look at financial experts' advice so you can improve your finances practically. Of course. I can also tell you from personal experience in money magic that one of the hardest parts is asking for what you actually want financially. Because I didn't. I used to do some kind of crazy, witchy math where you try to figure out how good of a person you actually are, how many favors you've asked, what bad deeds you've done, and do you actually need this? I was never going to step forward into bigger and better things with that intention. It's really fucking scary to ask for what you want. It's even more scary to get it.

When I was doing magical work to change my finances in 2012, A2 invited me to NYC with her to talk with an older gentleman on the Upper West Side out of an antique couch. A2 took me to the jewelers at the Waldorf Astoria and I remember being in love with The Bracelet with my little nose pressed to the glass. It was gold with gorgeous aquamarines, pink topaz, and yellow diamonds.

"So try it on," A2 said casually.

My palms started to sweat just at the *idea* of having a $25,000 aquamarine diamond bracelet on my wrist, even under the careful supervision of Stephen the jeweler. But I had gotten brave because we had just sweet talked our way into acquiring A2's antique couch. The older gentleman clearly had come from old money and I had never been in a NYC apartment anything like his. A2 knew about my magical financial work but also knew I was a weenie. I wore a white skirt from Anthropologie that I could barely afford on clearance and a matching (clearance) sweater. I accessorized with a handwrought bronze leaf necklace, a gift from a much more famous author friend. I had just bought a clearance Kate Spade bag that was embroidered with, "she is quick and curious and playful and strong." Jow was Not Thrilled at the time about said expenditures. We were new homeowners and we were terrified that if we breathed wrong, the condo would immediately collapse and then be foreclosed on.

"She's getting married!" A2 said conversationally to Stephen. I was about to be married to Jow. My second marriage. Another thing that made me want to throw up in my own mouth, since the first one was so stellar (as evidenced by being divorced).

I thought about my borrowed wedding jewels, my borrowed wedding dress, and my borrowed wedding shoes. All far nicer than I could ever afford. I was grateful to borrow them from A2. I thought about our homespun decorations. There would be no dancing, we couldn't afford it. Everything was changing so fast. But I knew I had two choices—to step forward and to be brave enough to ask for more than I thought I deserved, or to keep shrinking away from wonderful experiences being offered to me.

"I'd like to try the bracelet on," I said, trying to be brave. My voice only quavered a little. Stephen graciously agreed to let me not only try it on but also take a picture of it (which I have on my desktop to this day). "To show your husband-to-be," he said kindly.

I can honestly say that's the moment my life really started to change. It didn't feel like the Moment. Not then. I was still a nanny with an uncertain income and no retirement savings or health care. I could barely afford the martini at the bar at the Waldorf, it cost as much as breakfast *and* lunch at a diner. But I ordered it and drank it and it was damn good. I started to believe that maybe, just maybe, everything wasn't out of my reach.

Money doesn't magically fix everything, but it can fix a lot of things. Money isn't going to rain down from the sky (probably) from your magical and practical work, but you could get a raise, a promotion, a better career trajectory, a financially savvy friend who wants to teach you about how money works, clearance sales on things you would like to have. Maybe I don't exactly need the Bracelet, but I can still dream about it. Maybe someday I'll get it. I can work toward not thinking about money at the grocery store again. I can work toward new floors in our condo that don't fill me with rage and a new car for Jow, both by saving and doing magic. I don't need to deserve it and you don't either.

Fortuna Eruditis Favet

Yesterday I fell down an Ovid rabbit hole from which I didn't emerge for several hours in researching Fortuna. I wanted something classical in feel because

Latin = fancy! As I read more and more about her, I found that poets and play-wrights generally had mixed feelings at best for our girl; at worst, they were flat out antagonistic.

She *is* capricious. And clever. She has a *huge* list of titles. She's one of our mad girl scientists like the Moirai, which is part of my fierce love for her. She doesn't care if something hurts you, thrills you, delights you, brings you up, or brings you down; she's committed to the process. She's committed to the wheel. Her wheel. It turns, it turns, it turns.

Right now, during this difficult time, you are likely in the *sum sine regno* section of the wheel (I have no kingdom). The cheerful news is that every-one spends some time there. It's not a particularly fun part of the wheel but it's part of the process. The even more cheerful news is that the next section of the wheel is *regnabo* (I shall reign). From there it's onto *regno* (I reign) and then dourly onto *regnavi* (I have reigned), and then down into our current place in the mud. No one is excited about the *sum sine regno* part of the wheel. No one with any sense, at least. But it's inevitable. You've crashed and burned for what-ever reason and now here you are.

Part of how that happens is by recognizing when it's time to turn the wheel. The more you struggle against accepting the part where your reign has ended, the more vicious the next segment will be—you without a kingdom. If you accept when your reign has ended and figure out what you still have to depend on, it will be easier to turn the wheel. What do you need to do to move to the next segment? Fortuna doesn't want the wheel to stop; she's here for the wheel, not your feelings. If you try to stop the wheel to just have the good parts, she will throw you down herself. If you struggle against that lesson instead of trying to take it in, she's going to let you lie there face down in the mud contemplat-ing why you are a bad pony until you're ready to abide by her rules. Remember, she's a mad girl scientist, don't get in the way of progress.

Think: Amy Dunne from *Gone Girl,* think Bonnibel/Princess Bubble-gum from *Adventure Time*, Irene Adler from any Sherlock Holmes iteration. Wheels within wheels. If you can become close to Fortuna, understand the cycle of the wheel, fully immerse yourself in all the sections we travel through (all four sections over and over just in this one lifetime), you can exert some control over your wheel with Fortuna's help and hand. You can figure out how to spend as little time as possible in *regnavi* and *sum sine regno* and as much time as possible in *regnabo* and *regno*. More ladders, fewer snakes. Not to mention perhaps a bit more money along the way.

Turn the wheel.

Rite to Fortuna

In your ritual work for Fortuna, you will need to explain that you understand that both parts of the wheel will happen in your life. You do know that, right? Magic has a price, just like everything else, so we can't be surprised when it's our turn to pay it. Explain why you want her to help you turn the wheel and why you deserve to be brought up in her favor again.

Offerings to Fortuna

Think cornucopias overflowing with fresh fruit, vegetables, and plants; fleshy beets or charred bits of beef; earthy red wine or lush milk and honey. Verdant succulent plants. A variety of grains. Coins from around the world. Heady incense.

Invocation

(Based on parts of Ovid's *Ars Amatoria* from parts of book I, unapologetically reworked and reclaimed in the name of Fortuna)

rustic Modesty, begone far hence:

Fortuna favors the bold.

Crave her favor and you'll be an orator on your own.

Play the lover and enchant with your words

gain faith in your art.

It's not hard to be believed when you are sincere.

Now is the time to catch Fortuna's regard

as the hanging bank is eaten away by clear water.

Let us praise her fair face, her lovely hair,

her well-shaped fingers, and her dainty foot:

even maidenly goddesses need to have their beauty proclaimed.

For goddesses to exist is lovely and since it's lovely, let's think on it:

let incense and wine be offered on small hearths to Fortuna

To get what you want, ask! She only wants to be asked.

Fortuna's wheel will spin in our favor when she is praised and honored.

And so we give her incense, sweet words, and our requests.

Fortuna, we ask you, please hear us.

Lakshmi as Lady Luck

If your love life is lacking, if your wallet is empty, if you need a pure straight shot of luck, if you need glamour, if you need beauty, there is no one who can fix your situation better than Lakshmi. That doesn't mean she's standing around with her purse open, desperately hoping to give you everything you ever wanted. Your mom doesn't do that, Lakshmi doesn't either. She's known for her capricious nature and is fiercely independent. She also appreciates hard work, modesty, and bravery, and she's known to take off when you start slacking off.

Churning and Churning and Churning

Once, Lakshmi liked Indra, the warrior god. She helped him protect his cities through her influence. Indra got real salty about it, though, claiming it was through his prowess alone that protected the cities. Lakshmi liked Indra, though, so she rolled her eyes and put up with it until a sage offered him a sacred garland of jasmine. He tossed it on the ground and spurned the offering.

Lakshmi could put up with a lot from Indra, but disrespect for something so pure and genuine as an offering was not one of those things. She was *so* ticked off, she blinked herself out of existence so he could see how good he did without her. Spoiler: not good. Not good at all.

The world is literally crashing and burning in flames, and the other goddesses started to get anxious and they said to Indra, "Damnit, Indra. Now you've really put your foot in it. Now none of us are happy. What do we do?" Indra asks Vishnu how they can put the world back together. Vishnu says that they're going to need to churn the ocean of milk all together. He, Vishnu, says something along the lines of, "It's gonna take a thousand years though, bro. So, get comfortable. You know how she is. But everything's gonna be good again, we just have to stay focused. Oh yeah. We need to talk to the ocean, too, so we can make sure we can get this all sorted."

All the goddesses got together and while there were many other side-adventures during this thousand years (an elixir of life, an immortality potion, something about demon slaying), they stayed focused and churned the ocean of milk for a thousand years so Lakshmi would come back and see that they were all really super sorry. Thus, satisfied that everyone was now really, really sure again that they needed her, Lakshmi made her grand entrance from the ocean of milk back into the world. She told Indra to piss off in exacting, long-form detail. Then, she chose Vishnu as her husband because he really got her and was willing to put in the work. Unlike Indra, who did not.

A Puja Rite to Lakshmi

If you haven't already, go back and read the parts about Agni and Ganesha from Durga's puja section, as they will apply here too.

You will need:

Two small fireproof bowls

Two potholders

A picture of Lakshmi you have either bought or printed from the internet, ideally in an inexpensive frame

Kumkum powder (you can make this yourself; search "DIY Kumkum powder" online)

1 T ghee (You can make this yourself; search "DIY Indian Ghee" online.)

A bell dedicated to puja rituals

Sweets (Search the internet for "Rose Burfi Recipe" if you want to be fancy about it. If you have a local Indian bakery, she'll be happy with anything there. Packaged Indian sweets from a Desi market are also generally well received, as is dried fruit.)

A small plate for the sweets (Read about *prasad* in the ritual instructions.)

Cotton wick (Search the internet for how to make cotton wicks for puja.)

Small cup like a shot glass

Good quality milk

A lighter

Small colorful roses

A vase for the flowers

Incense (I find she's partial to rose) and an incense burner

½ a camphor tablet

Tiny picture of Ganesha in a picture frame

A smaller amount of sweets for Ganesha, in front of his picture

Mala beads (It's best to dedicate each set of mala beads to each specific goddess you work with whenever possible.)

Before starting, set up your altar area with Lakshmi and Ganesha's pictures. Follow the altar set up as previously outlined in Durga's puja.

1. Start by facing the picture of Lakshmi. Turn in a circle clockwise, clapping your hands eight times for the eight directions as you turn.

2. Ring the bell. Announce the date and time and your intention (e.g., "I am here to perform a puja for Lakshmi").

3. Acknowledge first Ganesha for being awesome and removing the obstacles. He always is thanked first before any actual puja activity starts because of the race he won against his brother and his parents decided that's how things should be going forward, as previously mentioned.

4. Light the wick. When lighting it, thank Agni for being there as fire and acting as a gate. Light the incense and camphor.

Lakshmi Puja Set-up

5. Tell Lakshmi about the sweets, milk, flowers, and incense you got her.
   Show all of these things to her by holding them up to her picture's eye
   level. In your own words, tell her how awesome she is. Tell her why
   you want to work with her and ask for her help. Say her seed mantra: *Om Shrim Maha Lakshmiyei Namaha* (ohm SHREEM mah-ha
   Lock-shmee-yah nah-mah-hah) "Salutations to the goddess who protects me!" You can look the mantra up on the internet if you're not sure
   about pronunciation. It's not required, but it's good brownie points to
   say her mantra 108 times, using the mala to keep count as we discussed
   previously.

6. Put some kumkum powder on the picture (on her head and feet) and
   then take a little off the picture and put it in your hair. Kumkum powder stains, so be careful.

7. Thank Ganesha for his presence. Thank Agni for his presence. Thank
   Lakshmi for her presence.

8. Ring the bell.

9. As in step 1, move in a clockwise circle and clap your hands facing all eight directions. Say, "This puja has ended but I welcome your company if you want to stay."

10. ***Very important:*** You *must* eat some of the food you gave her or she will think you gave her garbage, which is incredibly offensive to Hindu deities. This practice is called *prasad*. If you give flowers, some flowers must be given to others. If you gave sweets, eat some of them. It's also encouraged to share these offerings with other people to share the experience of being in Lakshmi's presence.

The Universe's Hidden Couch Money

This section will be primarily Hoodoo-based because Hoodoo tradition understands the need to pay your electric bill every month. Sometimes you need a bit of money fast. I have generally found it difficult to shake out large amounts of money this way but have found enough to put food on the table and pay an unexpected bill. Obviously, consider practical matters as well. Can you get a side hustle of some kind? Can you work an extra shift? Can you sell something? Have you looked into local resources that might be able to assist you? Magic can help you step through the door, but you have to open it first. All of these little suggestions can be done individually, mixed and matched, or all together, whatever your personal preference happens to be. There's no particular order here.

- Get a quarter coin from every working adult in your household. Put them in a shot glass. Put a mirror under the shot glass to magnify the effect. Cover the coins in honey and fill the glass with it. Set your intention to bring money to your house over it. Clean it out and replace it with new honey periodically.

- Get two lodestones that are magnetized to each other. Feed them gold filings on a weekly basis by sprinkling filings on the stones.

- Get a High John root. Feed it weekly with High John oil by sprinkling the oil on top of it.

- Glue a mirror onto your stove so that it reflects your burners, which will bring you prosperity.

- Keep a cedar tip in your wallet.

- Etch symbols and words that are meaningful to you into a green candle. Dress it with cinnamon oil and dab the oil in the direction that moves toward you. Light it off your stove if it's gas. If you have an electric stove, a match is fine. Burn a new candle weekly.

- Get a fresh whole pineapple. Cut off the top leaves and set them aside. Cut the pineapple into five pieces. On each piece, drizzle honey, cinnamon, and ginger beer. Stick a dollar (or a quarter if you can't afford the dollar) to each piece. Stack the pieces up and burn a gold candle on top of the pieces. Drench the leaves in the best perfume samples you can get your hands on. When the candle has burned out, put the leaves on top. Leave out overnight and discard in the morning.

The Pit of Vipers, Your Workplace

In my previous workplace, the moment you put me in a seminar where we are asked to talk about our workplace difficulties, everyone's response is always that I should look for another job. The exception was always the instructors who have seen enough to know better. It's not actually a helpful response to many of us in a difficult work environment. It is such a dated, privileged thing to offer advice to a person about work or home life decisions when you don't have all the information; I immediately lose respect for the other person when it's said. *Zomgoats, Betsy! Thank god you have distilled my incredibly nuanced problems at work and/or home down to such an easily managed proposition that I totally have not thought of! I would have never, ever thought of leaving if you didn't point out to me that that's an option! You are such a godsend. Nay, savior.*

Sometimes, all we can do is learn to endure. Many of us weren't taught that about the workplace, but it can help us get through the hard times. But that doesn't mean you have to just sit there and take it. Yes, you will sometimes need to appear as a supplicant to survive in the workplace. That said, it doesn't mean you shouldn't have a plan past *ALL OF YOUR JOKES ARE SO FUNNY AND YOU ARE SO ATTRACTIVE AND SMART*. It doesn't mean that you shouldn't have an end date for yourself in dealing with these shenanigans. You need to do more than just get through the day. You know what practical things you are supposed to be doing. Find out what your options really are for escaping by arranging your finances, looking into secondary income streams, getting your physical appearance in order for interviews (it matters there), talking to professionals as needed (therapists, lawyers, accountants, stylists), and doing what you need to do. Figure out what you need to be happy. Really happy, not socials happy. Start making that happen.

Then, get your magic in order. Trouble with someone wielding power over you and being a jerk about it? Hit up your recent ancestors, the ones who remember you as a tiny adorable baby, who always cheered for you, and who always slipped you a twenty when you needed it. Tell them about your problems. Bring cake. Catch them up on the family gossip. Let them take care of things. If how they will take care of it worries you, ask them not to do X or Y. Or, leave it to them if you trust them like that.

Stop living like a filthy hamster at work, it's not good for you. Wipe down all your surfaces with antibacterial cleaning products. Keep your work area neat so you don't attract everyone else's garbage energy.

If you have little actual personal space to call your own in the workplace, think small and do what you can get away with. Think vaguely office appropriate New Age décor that you will obviously do lots and lots of magic to at home. Anoint the objects, do moon-phased timed rites, cover them in crystals and herbs, whatever your thing is to get an object to work for you magically. Do these things at home, which (hopefully) is not a toxic cesspool like it is at work. If it is, go outside.

Consider a salt lamp. It can actually do something for the air, it's only minorly weird and it's a huge hunk of salt to banish negative crap from your space. A small Resurrection plant never hurts to have either. In my last workplace, I bought myself a clear glass ramekin and a Resurrection plant (obtainable online or at the local Witch shop). I also got a small round mirror and some rough rose quartz. You can use this for yourself in your workplace, too. Draw a meaningful sigil on the mirror. Surround the mirror with the rose quartz. Put the Resurrection plant into the ramekin with some water. The mirror and the rose quartz magnify all the positive vibes that you and your plant can muster. When your toxic awful work environment inevitably tries to drown you, it's okay! Let the water evaporate and the plant curl into itself. Then add more water and start again. Your plant is coming back to life! *What now, crummy workplace?* Not having sunlight is a great reason to give as to why there's a Resurrection plant on your desk. Plus, anyone with an Instagram account or a kid with one will just assume you are suddenly very fashionable. Whatever. Stop soaking up all the negative vibes into yourself like that is part of your actual job description and focus on what is actually in your job description and do your best to shield against the rest. Just because you are handed a bag of rocks doesn't mean you have to carry it, unless it's part of your job and you've agreed to that already.

If workplace gossip is a problem, start practically. Invite suspect(s) out to lunch. Don't bother trying to address the issue because in all likelihood it would instead be an exercise in blame-storming. It can be difficult to get to the root and even harder to know what anyone's intention actually was. Assign a reason about why they are gossiping if that makes you feel better and then leave that aspect alone because it's all just speculation anyway. During lunch, just be as *charm*ing as you can be, if you know what I mean. Think old movie charming like Audrey Hepburn or Spencer Tracey. Project an energy of likableness. Be as fun and outgoing as you can be, and then the suspects may think more kindly toward you because of that energy. Or maybe because you both like *The Real Housewives of New Jersey,* whatever. The whys matter less than the results here. When possible, offer to do the crap jobs that no one wants to do, whatever they are in your office which will also curry favor typically.

Then, literally break bread with your coworkers. Bake something. A quick-bread, cupcakes, brownies, a box mix, whatever. Just be sure you add Stop Gossip Spice Mix to it. In a coffee grinder, grind up the following to a fine powder: 1 piece whole cinnamon, 3 cloves, 1 teaspoon allspice berries, 1 teaspoon brown sugar. Add 1 heaping tablespoon to your baking project. As you stir the batter clockwise, put your intention into it. The brown sugar is important because it will sweeten their dispositions toward you, the cinnamon is for fast action, the cloves are to stop gossip, the allspice is for good fortune in business and money matters. As you are baking your project, focus on putting your intent into it, that these people will like you and be favorably inclined toward you in business matters. Bring it to work the next day and offer the project to everyone who is giving you a problem, coworkers and your superiors alike. Leave what's left in the break room.

Finally, it's time to get a girl. It could be a favorite ancestor, a spirit you especially like, a goddess you already work with, or St. Martha. I love St. Martha because I really relate to her: she has a pain-in-the-ass sister (Mary Magdalene, whom I also love), and they fight like sisters do; only they can get Jesus Himself to referee. She is the one doing the dishes because apostles are messy and, god forbid, she complain about it. She goes to France with her sister and brother to tame a dragon because who else could manage that but Martha? You want someone who gets sloppy, messy workplace problems? She's your girl. She knows all about dealing with difficult people and working to keep the show on the road. Get a candle, look into her novena, and get to it.

You can also make a honeypot with the intention of sweetening your workplace (and the people in it) in your favor. In case you aren't sure, this is a moral compass question for you: Do you feel badly about working your will over others? This is probably not for you, then. Get a small jar of honey. Empty about a tablespoon of it into a small bowl. Put it on your altar as an offering and if you can, dispose of it by putting it by your workplace door (outside). Get a small piece of brown paper bag that will fit in the jar and write the names of everyone causing you problems three times. While you are writing, do not let your pen leave the paper—neatness doesn't count here, continuity does. Put on top of the paper three cloves (to stop gossip), three cardamon seeds (to attract good luck), and three chamomile flowers (from a tea bag if need be) to protect and keep money. Roll the paper toward you while setting your intention for job security, for the gossip to stop and for these people to be "sweet" to you (the purpose of the honey). Put it in the honey jar. Screw the lid on tightly and put the honey jar in your sink or cauldron (some place where it will be safe as we are about to get fire involved here). Now get a small green taper or chime candle and carve a symbol or words for your intention and put your will into it. Dress the candle with cinnamon oil (to make it happen quickly) using a motion to bring it toward you. Light the candle off your stove if it's gas, use a match in the kitchen if it's not. Let a little wax melt onto the lid of the jar and anchor the candle on top of the jar. Let the candle burn all the way down. Put the honey pot on your altar. Be sure to continue burning candles on top of the honey jar with symbols and prayers once a week to keep the mojo going. You are awakening a tiny spirit to do this work for you—if you forget to feed the tiny spirit, guess what happens? That's right, it dies.

New Career, New You

Finding a new career can be challenging as it requires learning new skills, navigating a new workplace, and figuring out what you want to do with this part of your professional life. What do you need to feel fulfilled? What makes you feel stifled? What kind of work environment do you like? What career could you see yourself doing if money wasn't an issue? Why? How much money do you need to make in your new field? Spend some time really thinking about these questions; read some books or online pieces and listen to some podcasts about changing careers. Start to outline what you would want and need. You could draw it, make a vision board collage, write about it in your journal, whatever usually works best for you. Once you have it down, clarify your thoughts about what you want in a new career into eight bullet points and write them out or print them on a Wednesday. Make an offering of sandalwood or lavender incense to Mercury. Praise is always a great idea as well. Then (on that Wednesday), make some Fire Cider Career Changer elixir.

Fire Cider Career Changer Elixir

A large clean mason jar

1 lemon, zested and juiced (for happiness)

1 T tumeric (for confidence)

¼ C fresh ginger, cut into large chunks (to heat things up and get things moving)

¼ C shallots, peeled and chopped into large chunks (to remove negative influences)

¼ C garlic, peeled and cloves kept whole (for prosperity)

1 t cayenne pepper (to remove obstacles)

¼ C honey (to sweeten potential employers toward you)

Good unfiltered apple cider vinegar (for vitality and wisdom)

Your written or printed intention

Yellow yarn, enough to tie around the mason jar eight times (to bring you happiness in your new workplace)

Keeping your intention in mind, put everything in the mason jar except the unfiltered apple cider vinegar. Fill the rest of the jar with the unfiltered apple cider vinegar. Screw the lid on. Shake it six times vigorously while thinking about your intention. Tie your intention (the eight bullet points) with yellow yarn around the jar, wrapping the yarn around the jar eight times. Tie it to the jar using eight knots. Shake the jar six times every day for a week, thinking about your intention every time (if you want to make this a longer project, you can shake the jar six times for six weeks). When it's Wednesday again, burn some more incense as offering and skim out all of the solid matter from the jar (the garlic, the shallots, the ginger).

Think about your intention. Pour yourself a shot of the elixir. Toast to Mercury. Every Wednesday, burn some more of the incense, have a shot of the elixir, and toast to Mercury until you have successfully transitioned into your new career. If you need to make more elixir, you can slip the yarn and your intention off the jar and either run the jar through the dishwasher or boil it in a large pot of boiling water for twenty minutes and then put the yarn and your intention on the jar again and make a new batch of the elixir. Once you have made the transition successfully, be sure to give Mercury thanks and praise both verbally and in offerings. If you have decided to go back to school for your new career, you can pause the ritual once you've gotten into a school for training and then resume when you begin looking for employment.

Pay Me

This work is to get a loan repaid or what you deserve to have in situations such as divorce or a death. This is another gray area spell because you are dominating that person's will with your own. If you don't feel comfortable with it, then don't do this spell. Obviously, you should also be taking actions such as finding a good lawyer, asking the person to pay you back, and getting an agreement in writing of what you are owed.

Have a picture of the person who owes you money along with some kind of representation of the money they owe you (e.g., a printed email you sent to ask for it, a copy of the bill they said they'd pay, your lawyer's business card). On a Thursday, start by putting together a plate of offerings to Jupiter. Offerings could include olives and figs, a small good bottle of olive oil or a very good bottle of port, possibly a fancy-looking Italian pastry like a *sfogliatella*. Make your offering (it will be discarded, not shared with humans) and explain what you need. Praise is always a good idea in this situation. Bundle the picture and the documents together, then get some cotton black thread and a good sturdy needle along with eight pieces star anise and eight juniper berries. Concentrate on what's owed to you and thread the star anise and juniper berries alternating. Wrap the thread with the herbs around the documents sixteen times while saying:

> I conjure thee, Jupiter
>
> God of storms
>
> I summon the
>
> force of your might
>
> Let us raise this storm together
>
> And may this storm follow [Name]
>
> Until I have received what I am owed

Put a bowl on top of the documents and put sixteen shelled walnuts in the bowl. Burn a purple candle every Thursday until you collect your debt. Thank Jupiter again when you do; making another offering wouldn't hurt here. Then leave the walnuts at a crossroads and discard the rest of the working.

Ten
Hexing

"I know we're on the brink of Civil War but I feel optimistic," A1 texted me. I knew what she meant. Some days during the pandemic, you are nothing but worries, huddled in your house wondering if you will receive your unemployment again because they are taking forever to update the system, if you will ever actually get a vaccine because every online scheduling system is erroring out, if you will ever see people you love indoors and unmasked again, if there are going to be more riots and unrest with the federal government change, if the school district will ever stop messing with the virtual schedule, if you'll ever get to travel again further than a couple hundred miles, worry, depression, worry, depression, worry, depression.

But then there are days where everything feels sort of okay. There are things to look forward to; you have plans to see people outdoors and masked which means you get to see loved ones in some capacity. It will someday be Spring again and that means outdoor dining and cocktails again. You'll be able to travel a little and get a small change of scenery, and you have learned to make *velouté de châtaignes*. You get to work out and maybe there's a change in federal government that could help us actually get vaccinated and help with civil rights. One day there will be tiny stitch-and-bitch meetups in your home.

There's no rhyme or reason to this, just as there's no rhyme or reason for starting to have good days. I remember this happening when I got divorced and when my father died. There were days when I didn't want to eat, when I would lie awake staring up at the ceiling, when I felt like nothing mattered. There were also days when I felt fine again. I could eat, I could sleep, I could laugh. It wasn't often brought on by anything in particular, the good days or the bad days, just my internal pendulum trying to re-calibrate itself. It's probably much the same for you and that's fine.

Once you start to have enough good days in a row, you can consider if you want hex work to be part of moving your life forward. You need to be in a place (ironically) where you're having more good days than bad days to consider this. You want to be mostly clear-headed, you want to consider if this is something you actually want to do. Hex work is delicate, as you will see in the coming sections. It requires a strong control over your will and for you to be pretty well grounded before you do any hex work. There's a little piece of advice I like to give when it comes to consuming alcohol or recreational drugs. You can always have more shots or marijuana later. You can take an hour or two between tequila shots or CBD-infused gummies. You cannot, however, have less later. If you only wait half an hour and then decide to double down with two more tequila shots or two more gummies, there's nothing you can do to stop the process if it's too much. You may vomit, you may have the spins, you may feel incredibly uncomfortable in some way, you may need to go to bed at the very sexy hour of 7:30 pm, and there's no way to undo that. If you waited two hours and decide one more shot or gummy could be a good idea because you don't feel much of an effect, it's much less likely you will get all those unpleasant side effects because you are making that decision more consciously and carefully. It's the same idea with hexing: you can always hex someone later but once you get that ball rolling, it's very difficult to stop.

That said, of all the people I have given this homily to, very few take the note. Instead, they wind up sick and regretful but got to learn it for themselves with visceral results. You may be someone who needs to learn for yourself too. All I can do is attempt to get you to assess your situation more slowly and carefully. If you don't take the note, then the consequences of your actions will be yours for you to wade through alone. I don't clean up other people's messes; few people will. Conversely, if you think hexing isn't for you and your moral compass, that's perfectly fine as well. I invite you to read this chapter anyway just so you have the knowledge in your brain, should you ever need it.

Your Moral Compass

Once, many moons ago, I was permitted to talk about hex work with my alma mater. That was not what was slated to be the discussion, but *apparently* if you make the vaguest mention of a book containing other things besides "love 'n light!!!!" to a group of bored college students, it's going to require further discussion. I took a moment to figure out where to start because generally there's not much discussion online about anything past technique and if there is discussion it's very *never ever ever ever ever.* And I don't really believe in never, ever, ever, ever. But I do believe in a moral compass. If it seems like I talk about this a lot, it's because I do.

When we were (are?) baby witches, many of us started with the idea of karma being something that's just waiting to come and get you the minute you step out of line. It's not a bad starting place, in certain aspects. You're learning a whole new belief system, you may have baggage from your old belief system, your frontal lobe may not be fully formed yet (mine wasn't!), you may be a rule follower (I was), so it's a reasonable starting point. But the truth is, karma doesn't work the way. It just doesn't. It's slow, it's accumulated over lifetimes (if we have many lifetimes, I'm not the person to give you a definitive answer on that point) and it represents both the good and the bad. And while the Law of Three is a nice idea that's meant to keep you from getting involved in some seriously dumb shit without thinking it through, it doesn't work in a way that's easily observable, if it works at all. In this life I have done things for good reasons that were actually harmful, and done things for bad reasons that were actually helpful. If it works for you, awesome. You are (still) captain of your own ship.

I can't tell you what the right thing to do is going to be for you. We don't have a definitive manual as Witches. There are no commandments (although our circle did use our founding mother's *thou shalt not* should *one's self* a great deal), many of our paths don't have a special moral code past *try not to be a jerk.* There's not even a really definite idea of what happens when we die for many of us, or a list of rules to follow like a lot of religions have.

If you haven't taken time to define your moral compass, now is a great time to consider it. If you have and it's been a while, it's a good time to reconsider it. Our values shift with age and circumstance. For many of us, we don't have to have a moral purview that's set in stone forever and ever. It's also important to be really honest with yourself in figuring out where your boundaries are. What are you willing to do magically and in life? Where is your line in the sand on what's too much? Whenever you work magic, you're forcing your will over someone or something. Do you need consent for you to do magic for another person? Does it matter to you if it's for healing that person or making that person fall in love with you or hexing them? You need to decide that.

Hex work is called a mess for a reason. I cannot stress that enough. I will say it again: *Hex work is called a mess for a reason.* Do *not* get yourself into a mess that you can't get yourself out of. I'm sure as hell not going to rush in to help you. Most people won't. Because it's *your* mess to clean up. Don't ever rush into curse work. If you're angry and not being sensible, it's not a good place to do curse work, you will likely do something you regret that will be difficult to undo. Always give it at least three days before taking action. Are you still mad after three days at that person? Then give it another week. Still mad? Give it another two weeks. Still mad? Maybe this isn't the right course of action for you right now. You might do it anyway. That's fine, but it's *your* problem and *your* choices that you will have to manage, no one else's, not even the person you want to hex! Do you want to tie yourself up further with the person you're angry with? Make no mistake about it, you *will* be tying yourself up closer with this person. Sometimes it will be worth it, sometimes it won't. Sometimes your magic will work in a way you won't expect it to. Often, in fact. Sometimes it will work better than you wanted it to.

While love spells aren't hex work exactly, it's all fun and games until you need to get a restraining order on someone because they desperately need to be with you. You need to think about if you want someone to be with you because they feel compelled to be. You need to make sure to do omen/divination work before you get involved with cursing so you can see if this is going to help or hinder you.

Make sure you are mindful about your personal concerns (your hair, blood, sexual fluids, fingernail clippings, clothes that you have sweated into or have any of your other fluids). Make sure you are mindful about collecting other people's personal concerns. When I once asked an auntie what to do if you don't have them, she calmly remarked, "But why wouldn't you?" If you're not willing to do what curse work asks, you're not really ready to take that step. And that's okay. It's okay if you never work a curse in your life. That's not what makes you a witch. Being in tune with where your moral compass is for your-self does. It's good to know the technique just in case, but it's also perfectly fine if you never use it.

On the other hand, for those who are now very excited for the chance to wield the dark arts, curse work is a "sometimes" food. One of my aunties and I have speculated that you get maybe three really good ones in a lifetime. You need to make sure they count and are justified when you do them if you want them to stick. If you curse all the time, it will likely come to consume you, which in turn will make you a boring person who is not good company. Also? I frankly feel exhausted just thinking about hexing every vague slight. You should have better things to do with your day. Revenge cycles in traditional literature exist for a reason, it tends to get you trapped too. There's plenty of research in psychology to indicate that while we think that revenge is going to give us closure, often what it actually does is put you into a cycle where you desire escalating retaliation, giving you the opposite of closure. Put more suc-cinctly as a friend once said to me as an early twenty-something, "He could be eaten alive by a pack of flaming dingoes and it still wouldn't be enough for you." He was absolutely right in that particular situation. Does that mean that if your moral code allows for hexing that it's never worth it? No. It does not.

Use a Flyswatter for Flies, not a Bomb

The first thing you need to consider in hex work is scale. I know it's *super* excit-ing to get to flex your magical muscles. Let's be real; most of us live lives that more closely resemble a less fun, less witty version of *The Gilmore Girls* rather than an episode of *Coven*. If you are living your life correctly, you likely rarely need to hex anything. You rarely should want/need to work on someone. I say living life correctly intentionally because if you need to hex all the time in your own life, you've made some wrong decisions about the people you have in your life and some poor life decisions that need to be evaluated on a non-magical level, possibly with a therapist. You are the common factor (and the only one you actually have any control over), not the other people.

But sometimes, someone you really loved and/or trusted really hurt you. Let's be real, that's what this is about. They hurt you, you want to hurt them worse. Quid quo pro. That's fine. Not everyone has New Testament leanings about turning the other cheek. How badly did they actually hurt you? Take some time to evaluate this both emotionally and intellectually. Did they salt and burn your fields or were they mean to you once? Did this person try to physically harm you? Did this person try to take away your livelihood? Did this person betray your trust and love in a way that is intentionally harmful?

Let's talk frenemies because they're always a fun time. Is this frenemy nice to your face but always talking shit behind your back? Are they spreading false rumors? Are they scheming against you in some way? Great. Maybe you need magic to deal with it. However, the first part of dealing with this person is acknowledging you're feeding into the toxic situation because part of you likes the drama (you do, or you wouldn't be doing it). So, you need to stop feeding into it as much as possible and distance yourself from them. Would a "Stop Gossiping" spell be appropriate? Yes. Would a "Freezing" spell be appropriate? Sure. Would a mirror box spell where whenever the frenemy talks shit about you, it gets reflected back onto the frenemy? Possibly, if you want to get a bit deeper into the woods. Do you need to get an intranquil spirit involved? I highly doubt it. If you overreact magically every time someone wrongs you, you're going to wind up with a mess. A really gross mess.

Is this just about feelings that will calm down in a reasonable amount of time? Betrayal stings is a giant understatement. But it's not just about that, you thought you and this person shared a reality. You thought you could trust and love each other. You thought you were on the same page. When this person betrayed you, you were forced to realize you're not even reading the same book. If that was a lie, what else is a lie? That's the headfuck, feeling like you don't even know how the world works as it reforms and reshapes around you.

Think about it this way: You really want to hurt this person, right? And you want it to count, correct? That's the purpose of the hexing, no? Do you want to be sobbing and impotently flailing at them trying to slap fight them into submission or do you want a pound of flesh? Do you *really* think if you can't even feel the ground under you that you will be able to be cunning enough to take that pound of flesh? Will you have enough control over your will and your magical ability in a state of shock? No. You will not. If you really want this to stick and you really want this to count, you will need enough self-control to wait until you have complete control over your will again.

Here's the thing about being betrayed, hurt, or otherwise damaged: It will never be enough. If someone has managed to really hurt you, and I mean *really* hurt you, there will never be a time where it feels like whatever vengeance you've exacted is enough. I had Your Standard Psycho Ex-Boyfriend in college. It was your Standard Bad Scene where he would stalk me and threaten to show up at my classes, at my workplace, at my home where I was alone—the usual psycho Sturm und Drang. However, I was still young and it was my first time with this level of romantic bullshit, so I was really damaged by this. It was really bad. I wanted him to suffer for all the nights I couldn't sleep, the sting of humiliation I felt for needing to be walked out to my car at night by coworkers, all the fear I felt as I constantly looked over my shoulder, unsure if he was there waiting to stab me nineteen times because that would sure show me how much he loved me. It was terrible. It was awful. In the end, my mommy had to call his mommy to tell her to check her son if she didn't want her kid served with a restraining order. His mommy reigned him in because I was not the first girlfriend this had happened with. Life went on. I wanted vengeance, but it was clear that nothing would ever be enough for me at that point in my life so I needed to just let go of it completely. Not forgive per se, but let go of. Forgiveness is optional in life as witches. If you want to, go for it. If you don't, you can take it to your grave. The trick there is learning to live with it without it consuming you.

Vengeance is tricky. It's sticky and it's not a straight line. It wants to pull you in, it wants you to be the cat playing with a slowly dying mouse. It wants to be your lover, your life, your reason for getting up in the morning, your perfect drug. But every time you hex someone, you are creating a stronger bond between you and that person. No hyssop powder or perfumes of Arabia will sweeten this little hand. It's okay to be willing to have that strong bond, it's okay to accept that as the cost of doing business here. But you need to assess if you will be consumed by it. The best and easiest way to keep from being consumed with it is to ask for what's fair. Asking for what's fair shows that you can be reasonable, even in this state. Be organized and sensible. Asking for raining frogs shows that you are a crazy person. You will either get what you asked for (yikes, in most cases) or be ignored. You don't want to be ignored and you don't want your crazy fantasies to come to life. Keep your wits about you.

Another aspect to keep you from getting completely consumed by this is to limit yourself to one working. Ideally, one that doesn't have to be fed for too long and something that you leave in the woods somewhere. Think about villains from James Bond movies. Were they effective? No. They had ridiculously complicated plans. Complicated is what messes everything up in vengeance. Keep it neat, clean, and quick. You will be unlikely to tell many people about what you did, so no one will admire your handiwork anyway. This is a magical hit. Get in and get out.

You need to work with your goddesses and spirits here, if you have those. They will be far more creative than you on your best day. Ask for fairness in your vengeance, keep your intention simple and neat. Ask them to enact it on your behalf. You don't need to lay out a complicated blueprint. Explain what was done to you, explain what you want to happen in broad terms and why. Then leave it alone. It's critical for you to leave it alone for your goddesses and spirits to work on this for you. It will often take a long time, longer than you would like in most cases. Let the Fates spin the web. Be patient, give it time.

Keep It Clean

Whenever you work any kind of hex against someone, no matter how big or how small it may be, always remember to physically shower immediately after with some lemon salt scrub. A recipe if you want to make it yourself would be one lemon juiced, 1 cup sea salt, ½ cup coarse sea salt. Mix together in a mason jar and seal it. Wash your hands and the bottoms of your feet with the salt scrub in the shower. Wash your hands with hyssop powder and burn some dried rosemary on a charcoal, letting the smoke wash over you and your home. You can't be cleansed entirely from your hex work, but you want as little residue left on yourself as possible.

Uncrossing

Let's get to the next exciting aspect of hex work. Is someone hexing you? Highly doubtful. God, wouldn't it be awesome if you were? It's easy to think that you are, especially during a difficult time. You have new enemies, everything is a mess, nothing makes sense. It's so much easier to take care of a potential hex than do all the boring uncrossing work. It feels so much better to blame one single person for all of your problems. When you know that someone is working on you, it's really easy to simply hit them back harder and fix it. Fix them, more to the point.

But sadly, rarely are any of us half as interesting as we would like to think we are. It's very doubtful there are malefica spells being cast in your honor. Because really, when someone takes the time to hate you like that, you are indeed very special and very dear to their hearts. I'm really serious about that. It's why they're trying to slowly drive you to death and/or madness with magic. You can't summon up that level of interest for someone whom you aren't passionate about. But rarely is anyone that into you. Because that's usually some internal shrine-building levels of devotion. But sure, let's first entertain that notion. If you cannot think of someone who has a Hamlet level of hate-on for you in three or less seconds, you're crossed, not hexed. Sorry/not sorry. But let's say you do. You might. Remember it needs to be current and active. Like unless that jerk from middle school is still cyberbullying you currently or actively (loudly) talking shit about you, they probably have moved on. Same with exes of all stripes. Draw an omen about it in your medium of choice. Do the signs point to yes? Okay, then let's take it off you. You can decide if you want to do something about it two weeks post-hex breaking. Bring a very fresh egg with you to the woods along with a spade. Dig a little hole. Whisper to the egg about all the shit they've been talking, plotting, and scheming that they've been doing and how it's directly affected you. Tell the egg this person's full name. Focus on putting all of this energy into the egg and out of you by carefully rolling the egg over your body. Once you feel all of the hex energy gone from your body and into the egg, hiss, "I cast this hex out of me in the name of God Herself!" And smash the egg into the hole. Fill in the hole with dirt. Walk away, being sure not to look back.

If I'm not likely to be hexed, then why is everything all messed up? Well, your conditions could be crossed. You know your conditions are crossed when you've lost all sense of time (yes, even in pandemic). You don't know what day it is, what time it is, or what time it is in other time zones when talking to friends.

It's just a complete vortex with time moving like it did when you were eight years old again. (So fast! So. Slow.) If your dreams are unusual for you, you may be crossed. If you remember your dreams and they are usually related to work or anxiety (missing teeth, being late for something, a presentation you forgot about, etc.) or a specific setting where you fly and you're having a lot of dreams that are not part of your standard deck, you could be crossed. Especially if you wake up feeling tired even though you're sleeping the same amount. If you are running into a lot of inconvenient things happening that could become much more than a minor annoyance, you could be crossed up. Think things like your dishwasher isn't working, now it's flooded your kitchen and the money you had earmarked for a much-needed mini-break now needs to be spent on a new dishwasher. None of this is world ending but it's really annoying. You could be crossed if many people in your inner circles are suddenly also going through hardship and injury seemingly out of nowhere. Generally speaking, as much as everything you are currently going through during this time of hardship is just awful, it's not uncommon that insult will be added to injury in the form of also being further crossed because crossed energy tends to breed together and multiple like gross little goblins. Finally, it never hurts to do some omen or divination work to check to see if your conditions are currently crossed. Given your current circumstances, they probably will be.

So, great—you know your conditions are crossed. Now what? It would be great if we had clarity about how you got here, but that's unlikely to happen. Since it's your conditions that are crossed, it's basically a butterfly effect cesspool that you're rolling around in. You can try to do divination to find all the threads of where it came from but it's likely just a mess of seven jigsaw puzzles thrown in a bag with twenty missing pieces. The who is contributing to your crossed conditions isn't that important at the end of the day. I know it feels like it should be or would be at this point, but it's not. If you were suddenly covered in poison ivy welts, the where you rolled around in poison ivy part isn't as important as immediately getting into a tub full of Aveeno bath treatment and calling your doctor to see if you need Prednisone to deal with this mess. Same situation here. The first step here in uncrossing is to accept the fact that you're not going to get to point your finger dramatically at a few people/spirits and be all, *j'accuse! Problem solved!* You're not going to be able to untangle this rat king much, if at all.

If it makes you feel better, assign blame a few places but don't really do anything about it because that just makes a bigger mess for you to clean up later. It might be unconscious if it comes from other people, it might just be that you're attracting more garbage since everything is already kind of a dumpster fire in your life at the moment, it could be a lot of things. It's not really worth getting yourself tied up in it more than you are currently. Next, you know how you feel completely and utterly demotivated right now? You know how you have zero desire to accomplish any of your goals because making the smallest, most inconsequential step feels like trying to run under water so why even bother, especially right now when your situation sucks so hard? You need to crush that right now, (gender neutral) sister.

The quickest way to uncross yourself is to tell the (Goddamn) Universe (Herself) to go fuck herself (...you don't have to use those exact words). But still, she appreciates that kind of moxie from such a tiny being. Tell her that you won't be slowed down by all of this petty shit and you're going to run faster just to spite her. If you hustle when it's hardest, the (Goddamn) Universe (Herself) will reply, "Well then, Tiny Being 937465465895969696962113, you sure have some fight in you, don't you? I want to see what kind of bitty solutions you're going to try to build since you are undeterred by every obstacle I throw in your path. Well done, you." Then, for at least a while, there is often help instead of more chaos and despair.

Now for the part that everyone hates. Since your life is currently a hot mess, unless you are a very specific type of person, your living environment (including your car if you have one and your work place if you have one) is probably also a mess. If disorder makes you want to scrub tile with a toothbrush, you probably have mess elsewhere and it's probably not physical. Work, keeping your kids in order, showering, all the places you usually hold together may feel like they are spinning out of control. If that's you, with despair showing up in those kind of places, work on those aspects that have been wilting and dying to uncross yourself.

If you are a slob in despair like many of us, you likely have some unwanted visitors who are couch-surfing in your house. While you were binge-watching

Netflix, inhaling Chex mix, taking endless internet quizzes, and playing video games, they got together and decided to combine their powers into something bigger and more useful to cross you up. Why? I don't know, spend a day with a cat or a toddler and then get back to me. Give them their spiritual equivalent of a pineapple by banishing them with your preferred banishing method or just flat out gobble them up like the witch you are. Take care of it. Then clean your house.

I can tell you from personal experience during stressful times such as craft show season, tax season, book deadlines, and other fun things that make me create mountains of dishes and laundry that I could not care less about, it does cross up my conditions hardcore. My conditions are at least a little crossed right this very moment as I'm writing because I can write or scrub baseboards. This will make cleansing my house even harder, so I have that to look forward to post-book. But, I will still have to take care of it, and so will you. You don't need to make yourself crazy; a little dust and a little clutter isn't going to bring all the rat kings to your house. But you know when you are living like a semi-civilized adult and when you are living like a first-semester college freshman. Prevention is key if you don't want to have to work way harder then you need to when banishing rat kings. Keep things neat. If you don't want any ants, maggots, roaches, or actual rats in your home, cleanness won't keep them out altogether but can keep their presence more manageable. You don't want rat kings nesting in your home whenever possible.

Now that your house is clean, cleanse yourself. Use a rosemary bundle (don't forget the bottoms of your feet), wash your hands with salt, take a cleansing bath, pull out any evil eye barbs that have found their way into you, use the Full Venusian Queen of Heaven rites or your banishing rituals of choice. You know you're uncrossed when life starts to feel vaguely normal again, which can be difficult during the challenges you are currently facing. You are grading on a curve here due to those challenges, but you are looking for things like regaining your ability to sleep, your ability to eat, your ability to do your daily functions, showering, and not being greeted daily with a new fresh hell of inconvenient new events.

Hexing as Social Change

First, make sure you actually want to tie yourself up in hex work (yes, even for social change). Yes! It's much more exciting on a Thursday night after a long shitty day of dispiriting news headlines to involve yourself in the dark arts rather than raise funds for nonprofits that support the social changes you want to see in the world. But that doesn't mean your actual best skill set in social change is actually hex work. If you are better at fundraising than hex work, you should do fundraising. Think about your skill set: Have you done previous hex work? If so, how good were the results? Have you ever done anything like phone banking or protest organization or volunteer accounting for a nonprofit? Did you have good results there? Everyone can throw a hex. Not everyone is a CPA or a lawyer. Niche skills are critical to social change.

If you are going to protest against a rally that supports the Nazi movement, be careful above everything else. Do some research online about what are the best current protocols to follow in case there is tear gas or arrests. If you are medically challenged in any way, check credible online resources to see if you are a candidate for being involved in this way or if there are other ways that would be better for you and your health. Make sure you still want to go.

If it's still the course of action that you want to take, at the rally pick some key players who are either seeming like figureheads or confirmed figureheads for this event. Confirmed is ideal, do some research. Throw the *malocchia* (the evil eye) back at them. I say back because they are throwing the evil eye at the world first. You can throw it right back, return to sender. Say that person's name, summon your will, and take all that hateful energy that person is building and throw it right back at them with your eyes. Stare them down. If you want to really be overt, spit on the ground after you throw it back.

If you want to do some work at home, choose some ancestors who are against Nazis. For example, my grandfather was an Italian-American who fought against his own motherland in World War II. He was a native Italian who went through Ellis Island to come to America. In the war, he was missing in action for a few days, though (thankfully) he was found. He believed in democracy and was against fascism. You know what he would be really not into? Neo-fascists breaking into the Capitol. He would not like that *at all.*

He's a good ancestor for me to work with in this. Think about if you have similarly minded ancestors. If not, you probably have spirits and goddesses who are against the systematic genocide of a people. There's also always a Mary (Our Lady of Fatima, Our Lady of Guadalupe, Our Lady of Sorrows, whomever your Mary is). Your Lady of Peace may be willing to throw down because of your relationship with her and the greater good for the world, but if you don't have a relationship it's like a stranger asking you to get into a boxing match for them. So, consider that aspect when asking.

Pour everyone a glass of red wine, yourself included. If someone doesn't drink, sparkling water would work nicely. Get some pastries from a bakery. If you don't have a bakery, make coffee cake or pound cake.

Eat and drink with your ancestors/Marys/goddesses/spirits. Catch up. Talk about world events, tell them who died, who got knocked up, whose kid is still a fuck-up, the usual. When you feel their presence, raise everyone's (ahem) spirits up with some music that would speak to your feelings about the current world events, ideally music they would enjoy as well. Ask for their assistance and then throw your curse. You may be saying, *but what do I say?* You have to be able to sleep at night with what you throw, not me. That's up to you, sport. Speak from the heart and be concise. Draw an omen and then go from there.

Minor Hexing

Sometimes you're feeling petty and annoyed, real talk. Especially when your current world is a new stressful place. Many times in witchcraft, we're told to rise above. I'm here to tell you that you do not have to. Does that mean your minor hexes are consequence-free? No, of course not. It's not consequence-free when you say something bitchy and petty during a meeting. But is it worth it sometimes? It sure is. This spell work is for those very times.

Freezer Spell

This particular spell is often presented in "positive vibes only!!!" manifestos. It's not actually positive vibes only. Any time you are working your will over anyone else without their consent or permission, you have started to wander away from *do no harm* or whatever, even if it's healing and you have the best intentions. Maybe *especially* if you think your intentions are good. Does that mean you can never ever do that? It depends on how your moral compass is set. You can want to magically leave a situation that is no longer working for you, you don't have to give notice to the other party. But know that when you do that, you are working your will on that other party. If you're okay with that, then go forth. If you're not, then don't.

The freezer spell is also only a good idea if you no longer want a relationship in any way with this other person. The entire point of this spell is to freeze the other person out. If you still live together, if you still work together, if you need to coparent together, if you still see each other all the time at your coven or social gatherings, you may want to consider if you want to do this work because one of you is going to feel much less welcome in these places (and possibly be asked to leave said places) and it could be you. If you are doing this spell, you need to be completely done with the other person and willing to accept that it could have negative blowback for you. You might be done enough with this party (and possible social/professional consequences) to not care and that's fine too.

Use a picture of this person (printed on regular paper) and get some black salt, two plastic freezer bags, tap water, and mugwort oil. Double bag the freezer bags. Explain to this person's picture why you need to have them frozen out of your life. Put the picture in the inner bag. Add the black salt and mugwort oil. Add the tap water. As you are sealing both bags shut say, "I am freezing you out of my life, [person's name]." Put it in the freezer. When you feel the person has been sufficiently frozen out, on the night of a waning moon, dig a small hole outdoors and pop the frozen cube in the hole and bury it. Don't look back. Toss the freezer bags in the trash.

Cut and Clear

While the purpose of a cut and clear spell is more for you to stop obsessing over a person and to clear your conditions to move forward, it is still cutting ties from this previous relationship. Meaning, yes, you are once again working your will over another person to completely cut ties. Even if they left already. This work is often done when the person has already left your life but you haven't been able to move on and move forward yourself yet. Get a lemon, some sea salt, red thread, a paper picture of the person, and a knife. Tell the picture of the person why you are done with your relationship with them and any ties you may have to them. Cut your lemon while saying, "I am cutting all ties to you, [person's name]." Dip each half of lemon in salt. Take half of the lemon and tie the person's picture to the salted side with the red thread, wrapping the lemon half nine times. Wait until dark and go outside with a small shovel and both halves of the lemon. Dig a small hole and drop the lemon with the picture in it. Cover it. Don't look back. Before crossing the threshold of your house, squeeze the other salted lemon half over the threshold and say, "I have been completely severed from you, [person's name]." Step over the threshold.

Time Out

Sometimes, a person just cannot keep your name out of their mouth and it can really start to irritate you. For whatever reason, you want this person to stay in your life, despite this. Life is complicated, so is hexing. Get this person's current profile picture from social media. Print it on paper. Fold it three times away from you with seven cloves in it. Get a small black candle and carve that person's name into it. Anoint it with clove oil with a motion that moves away from you. Drip it onto the paper while saying, "For as long as you keep spreading rumors and bad vibes about me, [person's name], I have you in time out." Put the little packet somewhere facing the wall until that person stops. Don't engage with this person any more than is absolutely necessary while they are in magical time-out. When the person stops misbehaving, say, "I release you from time out, [person's name]" and discard the packet using your method of choice.

Minor Jinxes

Sometimes, you're just really annoyed with someone and you want to annoy them back in some way. This is perfect for people you can't actually sever from your life. Minor jinxes are great for that. Pull up their profile on their social media and whisper to their profile page all of the minorly inconvenient things you want to happen to them throughout their week. This is where creativity counts in your conjuring. Some suggestions: May your Wi-Fi be down in your home for the next three days, may you never find street parking in a city, may your next sexual partner only be okay in bed, may your kids whine constantly until the next full moon, may every local store be out of your preferred brands, may you be stuck making small talk in the work place and unable to accomplish work for the next day, may your dog need to go out at 2 a.m. for the next week, may your cats poop outside their litter boxes in hard to find places, may you spend a lot of time getting ready and receive no compliments, may your next ten social media posts receive no likes and no comments.

Major Hexing

This kind of hex work isn't for when you are somewhat annoyed, it's for when you have been majorly wronged. It should also be for when you don't want a relationship with someone. So here's a hint: if you want a conscious uncoupling a la Gwyneth Paltrow where you and your ex are friends and go on vacation together with new partners and the kids like one big happy family, this is not what you want to do. If you were going to present a court case about this to a panel of judges from both your goddesses, spirits, and ancestors *and* the other person's goddesses, spirits, and ancestors, do you think you would win the case? If so, you can consider proceeding. If not, it would likely be unwise to proceed.

Spell Bottle

Enlist the help of your own personal goddesses, spirits, and ancestors, especially those who will likely be sympathetic to your case. Make them offerings. As previously discussed at length, you're not supposed to be doing this often, so make sure they're good offerings (or one half of a good offering with the promise of the second half upon delivery). If you don't do deities, offer to the Universe or whatever feels acceptable to you. State your case to them and state your intention. Be specific enough about what you want (justice, reparations, and so on) and why, but leave some room for your goddesses, spirits, and ancestors to get creative.

Get a bottle. If there is a kind of booze/beverage your opponent hates, so much the better. If not, use a bottle that has a witchy name (Black Toad beer, Hex beer, Strega liquor, Left Hand beer, etc.). Pour out the contents as a libation to your spirits.

Add nasty things such as nails, needles, broken glass, vinegar, hot sauce, hot peppers, and bits of items that the person hates.

You need a good personal concern from your opponent for this level of hex. Not a picture or handwriting, something good: blood, spit, hair, or sexual fluid. If you didn't have the foresight to have some of that on hand before the work and/or you don't have the chutzpah to find a way to get it, you have no business performing this level of hexing. Add it to the bottle along with your intention following the usual protocol of not allowing your pen to leave the paper as you write it and folding it away from you.

Seal the bottle up tightly and then piss on it.

Shake the bottle once a day every day for three days while asking your spirits for their help in what you want to happen. Don't phone it in—you want this to stick, so you want to feel moved by your own words so that your spirits will be moved as well.

Take it to the woods and hang the bottle upside down in a tree. Walk away from it and don't look back. It could take a while for this to work. Possibly up to a year or even longer depending on how many wheels need to be set in motion. Be patient. You'll know when it worked.

Mirror Box

If you are doing heavier hex work, you always want your goddesses, spirits, and ancestors involved to help you. Like in our other example, you want to give a major offering, state your case, and then give them some room to work. If you don't work with deities, spirits or ancestors, focus toward the Universe or whatever feels right for you.

Make a very small poppet of the person, dressing it with personal concerns. If you aren't super crafty, do an internet search for a tutorial on how to make a worry doll or a Waldorf clothes doll. Again, you need a good personal concern from your opponent for this, as previously defined. You cannot do this kind of hex work without it.

Get a small wooden box from a craft store. Glue tiny mirrors from the craft store inside the box. You want to cover the entire inside of the box with the tiny mirrors. Bind the poppet up with some string and tell the poppet why you are mad at the person. Tell the person that every time the target speaks badly of you or works against you that their words and actions will be reflected back at your opponent. Your moral compass may find this justified. If this person wasn't actively trying to damage you, nothing would happen to that person. At the same time, if this person doesn't stop working against you, it is sometimes said that it could cause this person to have a complete meltdown and possibly be ruined. You may feel justified in that as a possible outcome. If you do, proceed. If you don't, then don't.

Put the poppet in the box. Go to the woods. Find a large rock or brick and put it on top of the box and put the heel of your foot on top of it. Say, "I have you, [opponent's full name] under my heel." Walk away, don't turn back.

Shut Your Damn Mouth

It is once again ideal to make offerings to your goddesses, spirits, and ancestors for this. If that's not your thing, the Universe or whatever you feel called to work with. A paper with their name will suffice but as always, better personal effects will give you better results. You will need a beef tongue (Amish and Jewish butchers will have them, as do many Asian and Latinx grocery stores), black thread, a sturdy sharp needle, brown paper, red pepper flakes, cloves, licorice root, vinegar, and a jar. The beef tongue is not optional for this kind of work. If you don't feel comfortable with using a beef tongue for any reason (including being a vegan or vegetarian), I invite you to consider using minor jinxing or a time out instead.

Write the person's name three times on the brown paper following the usual protocol about your pen not leaving the page. Write "shut your damn mouth" three times across their name, again pen not leaving the page. Dust the paper with red pepper flakes, cloves, and licorice root. If you have personal effects, put them in there too. Fold it away from you three times. Cut a slit in the beef tongue wide and deep enough that will fit the folded petition paper. After shoving the paper in the slit, sew it closed while focusing on this person shutting their mouth tight when it comes to you. Put the tongue in the jar. Cover it with vinegar so that whenever they say or do sour things toward you, sour things come back to that person. When you feel that person has learned their lesson, go outside on a dark night during the waning moon and empty the jar's contents into a hole you've dug and bury it. Cover the hole and walk away without looking back. Recycle the jar, don't reuse it.

Epilogue

We are starting to come close to a year of pandemic life. I have a very specific memory of my last night before the pandemic began in earnest. It was tax season, the wheel of deadlines that controlled my life for the last five years. G. had an extra ticket to see *Six: The Musical* on Broadway, an evening show. I had gotten to see it in the West End in London last summer and Jow and I got to see it in previews on Broadway. We counted out the tax season social math together, to figure out if I could even take the ticket. It was during the week, which meant that it may as well been on Mars during tax season, but we are close enough to each other that I could be plain in my litany of demands—*I need you to pick me up at work at 4:45 p.m. and take me to the post office. We can leave from there. Don't come inside the office, we'll never get out. We can go to dinner before the show and a very quick drink and be home by about 11 p.m. This is late and dangerous because if anything goes off the rails, I could lose a day's work and they will want to murder me. I need you to drive. I need you to drive me home. I need Jow to take me to work the next morning because my car will be there at the office. But tax season is another six weeks of being locked down. It's worth the risk for this.*

She was on board. I decided to go.

We went to a beautiful Mediterranean restaurant that was all crisp white ropes and walls with cerulean blue blown glass. It was *just* fancy enough that usually I would prefer sitting at the bar than the fuss of a full-service meal, but it was tax season and the fuss felt good. It was as close to Holly Black's vision of fairy food I am likely to ever get to without a whole lot of effort. There was beautiful ceviche served with head and tail strewn with pansies, microgreens with spicy mandarin, farro paella with prawns so giant and juicy that I felt slightly bad that

173

I didn't fight them to the death first, and an assortment of fresh-baked baklava redolent with honey. We didn't know the words past "baklava," so we called them "hay bales," "round guys," and "regular guys" when discussing them.

We headed over to *Six* and it was everything I hoped it could bloom into during previews. Fresh, funny, sharp, amazing outfits, and voices as well as a sometimes painful commentary on how few of our struggles have changed with so much time. We were delighted.

After, I gave G. my "I'm such a party" talk which went something like "Okay, we can go drink rose booze punch out of teacups a block away but one drink only and you're not one of those lightweights who needs like an hour after one drink before she can drive, right?" Again, we're close, she knew what she was signing up for. She was just happy to get rose-St. Germain-vodka-burlesque bitters punch out of a floral teacup so she's amenable. The bar was bustling and lit mostly by candlelight. We drank our teacups full of boozy punch and talked and toasted. As I drank the last sip of my cocktail, I got that feeling I sometimes get when everything aligns perfectly for a long breath. It feels like being infinite.

I think about that night all the time. If I had known it would be the last time I would step foot in NYC in a year, I would have insisted on three teacups of punch and probably would have been needed to be pulled off the bar top and carried back to the car by G. But we didn't know, not really.

I should have had three of these.

Today, I have a scheduled vaccine. I don't know if it will actually happen, but it's a date. Jow is fully vaccinated and his nurse life has mostly slowed to its usual breakneck speed, though there are still cases. Soon, he starts work in Hospice. So far, after the Capitol protest went terribly off the rails, there hasn't been any significant unrest. It's so cold in winter, it's hard to be outside for much. I have a new (used) car. I attempt to help my nephew on his virtual school days. We do yoga together. He's getting good at warrior poses, but he also likes to flop around like a fish on his mat, mostly. Sometimes, I have one or two friends over. For my birthday, there was a heated outdoor igloo with boozy hot chocolate and a sushi boat full of fried food with my bestie. It was as good as I could hope for, but still I would wistfully think about earlier times, our house so full of friends and family, everyone eating and drinking and laughing until far too late.

It's hard to say where anything will be, over this next year. We've learned to measure in the space of a year, not days or weeks or even months. But that thread of wild hope that started to unspool for me on New Year's Day keeps winding its way around my heart, reminding me that magic is always possible, even when it's hard to see, it's still there.

I hope it's still there for you, too.

Postscript

Beatrice: I love you with so much of my heart that none is left to protest. (*Much Ado About Nothing* 4.1.78)

I finish this book's edits on a windy Walpurgisnacht. I want you to know that I'm thinking about you and your troubled times tonight, right now. And I'm sending you my love and, as my circle would have said, healing energy. For a long time, I thought the healing energy was a bit bullshit. Very, "thoughts and prayers!!!!" What was that going to do for me? A lot, it turned out. It did so much within our little circle, which is why I'm sending it to you right now. Maybe you're reading this with your heart broken, five years from now, the pandemic (hopefully) a distant memory, maybe you just lost your job and your field is dying, maybe your health is not doing well, maybe you've just lost someone very dear to you. I'm holding space for you, right now, on Friday, April 30, at 6:41p.m. EDT. I'm thinking about all of your future sorrow, all of your uncertainty, all of your hardship, feeling like you are free falling and you'll never find solid ground again. Everything is not magically all better right now in this place, in this moment. Not even for me. And probably not for you, even if you read the entire book and did every single piece of magic presented. But that's because nothing is ever all better. But it can be a little better. Breath by breath, day by day. The process is never finished until you breathe your last breath and I find that soothing, just as I have found writing this book to be healing. I've found it to be healing to do the magic I've given in this book, telling you to do the daily work has helped me to do the daily work myself and there were definitely some days through this crazy year that I didn't want to. I didn't want to get out of bed. I didn't want to do the work. I didn't want to do the magic. I didn't want to do anything but hope to go back to sleep. You, reading this book some day in the future, has kept *me* sane during one of the most globally turbulent years that have happened while I've been on this planet. I've shown people that I love this part or that part of this book to get them through their troubled times, even if was just to help them move forward through their day. There will be hope again for you. It probably doesn't feel like it right now. And it probably shouldn't. Because being present with your grief is what helps you move through it. Tiny piece, by tiny piece. Moment by moment. Maybe not this moment, maybe not the next moment, maybe not for many moments. But eventually, hope will return. I promise.

Recommended Reading

Amos, Tori. *Resistance: A Songwriter's Story of Hope, Change, and Courage.* Atria Books, 2020.

Brown, Brené. *Braving the Wilderness: The Quest for True Belonging and the Courage to Stand Alone.* Random House, 2017.

Chödrön, Pema. *When Things Fall Apart: Heart Advice for Difficult Times.* Shambhala, 2016.

Doughty, Caitlin. *Smoke Gets in Your Eyes: And Other Lessons from the Crematory.* W.W. Norton & Company, 2015.

Doyle, Glennon. *Untamed.* Random House, 2020.

Elliot, Susan. *Getting Past Your Breakup: How to Turn a Devastating Loss into the Best Thing That Ever Happened to You.* Da Capo Lifelong Books, 2009.

Fern, Jessica. *Polysecure: Attachment, Trauma and Consensual Nonmonogamy.* Thorntree, 2020.

Fisher, Carrie. *Princess Diarist.* Penguin, 2016.

Harrington, Lee, and Mollena Williams. *Playing Well With Others: Your Field Guide to Discovering, Exploring, and Navigating the Kink, Leather, and BDSM Communities.* Greenery Press, 2012.

James, John W., and Russell Friedman. *The Grief Recovery Handbook: The Action Program for Moving Beyond Death, Divorce, and Other Losses including Health, Career, and Faith.* William Morrow, 2017.

Katagiri, Dainin. *The Light That Shines through Infinity: Zen and the Energy of Life.* Shambhala, 2017.

Kendall, Mikki. *Hood Feminism: Notes from the Women That a Movement Forgot.* Penguin, 2021.

Kondo, Marie. *The Life-Changing Magic of Tidying Up: The Japanese Art of Decluttering and Organizing.* Ten Speed Press, 2014.

Lawson, Jenny. *Furiously Happy: A Funny Book About Terrible Things.* Macmillan, 2015.

Lorenz, Theo. *The Trans Self-Care Workbook.* Jessica Kingsley Publishers, 2020.

Mardell, Ashley, and Amy Melissa Bentley. *The ABC's of LBGT+.* Tantor, 2017.

Pittman, Catherine. *Rewire Your Anxious Brain.* New Harbinger Publications, 2015.

Schwartz, Arielle. *The Complex PTSD Workbook: A Mind-Body Approach to Regaining Emotional Control and Becoming Whole.* Althea Press, 2017.

Tawwab, Nedra Glover. *Set Boundaries, Find Peace: A Guide to Reclaiming Yourself.* TarcherPerigee, 2021.

Wiking, Meik. *The Little Book of Hygge: Danish Secrets to Happy Living.* William Morrow, 2017.

Selected Bibliography

Adams, Peter Mark. *The Game of Saturn: Decoding the Sola-Busca Tarocchi*. London: Scarlet Imprint, 2017.

Anderson, Cora. *Fifty Years in the Feri Tradition: Tenth Anniversary Edition*. Portland, OR: Harpy Books, 2005.

Balz, Dan. "After a Year of Pandemic and Protest, and a Big Election, America is as Divided as Ever," *The Washington Post*, December 27, 2020. https://www.washingtonpost.com/graphics/2020/politics/elections-reckoning/.

Beckett, John. "Why We Make Offerings," Under the Ancient Oaks, February 23, 2016. https://www.patheos.com/blogs/johnbeckett/2016/02/why-we-make-offerings.html.

Blackthorn, Amy. *Blackthorn's Botanical Magic: The Green Witch's Guide to Essential Oils for Spellcraft, Ritual & Healing*. Newburyport, MA: Weiser Books, 2018.

Buchanan, Larry, Quoctrung Bul, and Jugal Patel. "Black Lives Matter May Be the Largest Movement in U.S. History," *The New York Times*, July 3, 2020. https://www.nytimes.com/interactive/2020/07/03/us/george-floyd-protests-crowd-size.html.

Carrasco, David. "Sacrifice/Human Sacrifice" in *The Oxford Handbook of Religion and Violence*. Edited by Mark Juergensmeyer, Margo Kitts, Michael Jerryson. New York: Oxford University Press, 2013.

Chapin, Angelina. "Have You and Your Friends Had the COVID Talk?" The Cut, July 9, 2020. https://www.thecut.com/2020/07/friends-are -discussing-covid-19-rules-before-hanging-out.html.

Feuer, Alan. "Assaulting Officers, Illegal Guns and Unlawful Entry: Violent Protesters Face Federal Charges," *The New York Times*, 2021. January 7, 2021, updated April 29, 2021. https://www.nytimes.com /live/2021/01/07/us/capitol-building-trump.

Gary, Gemma. *Traditional Witchcraft: A Cornish Book of Ways.* London: Troy Books, 2008.

Gilbert, Elizabeth. *Big Magic: Creative Living Beyond Fear.* New York: River- head Books, 2015.

Harms, Daniel. *The Book of Oberon: A Sourcebook of Elizabethan Magic.* Woodbury, MN: Llewellyn Publications, 2015.

Larocca, Amy. "In a Pandemic, Is 'Wellness' Just Being Well-off?" *The Cut*, April 29, 2020. https://www.thecut.com/2020/04/wellness-during -coronavirus.html.

McCarthy, Josephine. *Magical Knowledge.* London: Mandrake Books, 2012.

Orapello, Christopher, Tara- Love Maguire. *Besom, Stang & Sword: A Guide to Traditional Witchcraft, the Six-Fold Path & the Hidden Landscape.* Newburyport, MA: Weiser Books, 2018.

Ovid. *The Love Poems: The Amores, Ars Amatoria and Remedia Amoris.* Trans- lated by A. S. Kline. Scotts Valley, CA: Poetry in Translation, 2015.

Parpola, Asko. *The Roots of Hinduism: The Early Aryans and the Indus Civili- zation.* New York: Oxford University Press, 2015.

Peterson, Joseph. *The Secrets of Solomon: A Witch's Handbook from the Trial Records of the Venetian Inquisition.* Scotts Valley, CA: CreateSpace, 2018.

Schiff, Stacy. *The Witches: Salem, 1692.* New York: Little, Brown and Company, 2015.

Solanaceae, A. *Saint Mary Magdalene.* Keighley, UK: Hadean Press, 2016.

Spinney, Laura. "Did Human Sacrifice Help People Form Complex Societies?" *The Atlantic,* February 27, 2018. https://www.theatlantic.com/health /archive/2018/02/did-human-sacrifice-help-people-form-complex -societies/554327/.

Starhawk. *The Spiral Dance: A Rebirth of the Ancient Religion of the Goddess: 20th Anniversary Edition.* San Francisco: HarperSanFrancisco, 1999.

Vaudoise, Mallorie. *Honoring Your Ancestors: A Guide to Ancestral Veneration.* Woodbury, MN: Llewellyn Publications, 2019.

Whang, Oliver. "What Is the Future of Black Appalachia?" *The New York Times,* September 26, 2020. https://www.nytimes.com/2020/09/26/us /black-appalachia-ron-jill-carson.html.

Zakroff, Laura Tempest. *Weaving the Liminal: Living Modern Traditional Witchcraft.* Woodbury, MN: Llewellyn Publications, 2019.

Index

To Write to the Author

If you wish to contact the author or would like more information about this book, please write to the author in care of Llewellyn Worldwide Ltd. and we will forward your request. Both the author and publisher appreciate hearing from you and learning of your enjoyment of this book and how it has helped you. Llewellyn Worldwide Ltd. cannot guarantee that every letter written to the author can be answered, but all will be forwarded. Please write to:

Deborah Castellano
℅ Llewellyn Worldwide
2143 Wooddale Drive
Woodbury, MN 55125-2989
Please enclose a self-addressed stamped envelope for reply,
or $1.00 to cover costs. If outside the U.S.A., enclose
an international postal reply coupon.

Many of Llewellyn's authors have websites with additional information and resources. For more information, please visit our website at http://www.llewellyn.com.